Never Give Up

A Father and Son Reunion
65 Years in the Making

Rex Beach

Never Give Up

Rex M. Beach

Published by Rex Beach
www.rexbeach.com
ISBN 978-1-68564-578-6

My Book is dedicated to my
two wonderful daughters
Ashley and Sarah Beach
and to my parents
Helen and William Beach

Contents

Introduction

At 7:45 pm on January 8, 2019, I was reunited with my father, who vanished in 1954. I was able to touch the container his casket was encased inside. My nine-year struggle to return his remains from an unmarked grave in Dallas, Texas, was over.

I said goodbye to my father less than forty-eight hours later as I gave him the military burial he deserved. On Sunday, January 13, 2019, the Associated Press carried the story about my father and me on the front pages of newspapers around the country.

My story is about my life after my father vanished in 1954 and different events that eventually led to finding my father and being reunited with him.

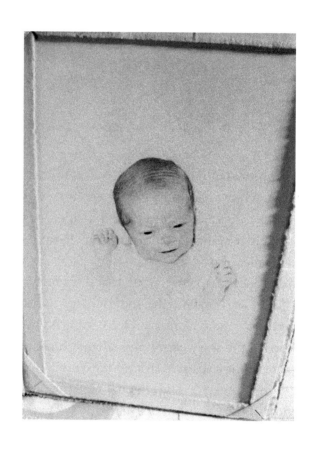

How it all began

~

These events were set in motion on January 24, 1948, when my mother and father, William Arnold Beach and Helen Covey, were married in Newport, Kentucky.

Sometime after their marriage, my parents moved to Dayton, Ohio, to live. For their first four years of marriage, they apparently were happy. I had one photo that showed my father sitting with my mother's family during one Christmas.

After four years of marriage, my parents decided to try and have a child. I was born on October 31, 1952, at 8.58 am, to William Arnold Beach and Helen Covey Beach, at St Ann's Hospital in Dayton, Ohio.

For the first two years, my parents lived an everyday life. My father was a furnace installer for the H.E. Noonan Heating Company. My parents lived in a middle-class home at 4750 North Main Street. Unfortunately, the house was torn down and replaced by a business many years ago.

My mother told me that I stopped breathing one day when I was a baby and turned blue. Since she was alone at the time, she called out for help, and a neighbor helped to revive me.

Dayton, Ohio, is known for more than being the birthplace of Orville and Wilbur Wright, who created the first successful airplane. In 1904 Dayton was the first city to issue a speeding ticket to a resident for driving twelve miles an hour. The rock and roll group, The McCoys, came from Dayton, and in 1965 their song, "Hang on Sloopy," became number one on the U. S. Billboard Top 100. The song was about a young girl from Steubenville, Ohio, a city 231 miles away from Dayton's town. The song was one that I would listen to many times as a teenager.

I could relate to "Sloopy"; I also came from a run-down part of town, and everybody tried to put me down.

Sometime after my second birthday, the love between my parents faded away. Life has taught me that love does not die overnight but slowly fades away with time.

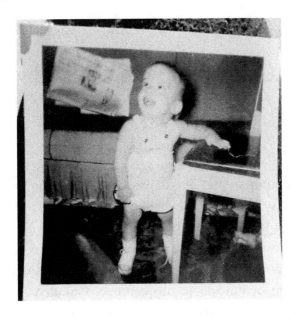

My mother's relatives knew my father for around six years. Nevertheless, they never told me anything about my dad or his family.

After my father left us, my mother told me that we moved from Dayton into apartments in a couple of small towns in Ohio near the West Virginia border. Since there were no daycare centers where we lived, she would drop me off at her parents' home when she went to work.

Growing up – childhood

My grandparents lived in a small town called Stewartsville, Ohio. They had a large three-story home built on top of a large hill. At the foot of the left side of the large hill was a large tunnel, which went deep into the mountain where coal was extracted. Around the turn of the nineteenth century, Grandpa Covey had his own small coal company. After a few years, he had to close the mine when the water was flooded by underground water.

When I was growing up, my mother told me that when she was a young girl, her father went to a meeting with a group of men who were members of the Ku Klux Klan. My grandfather took a stand against them and left the meeting.

One evening after that, my mother was using an outhouse, because their home did not have indoor plumbing or a toilet. While she was inside, she heard strange noises coming from outside. When my mother left to go back to the house, she saw a tall figure dressed in white, walking towards her with his hands stretched out, reaching for her. My mother ran inside, screaming.

When her father came outside, the man was gone. They assumed it was a Ku Klux Klan member trying to harass her father for not joining them.

There was a well in the backyard with a hand pump where we would get fresh water. There was a large yard around the home, and the property line ended at the edge of a forest. Grandpa Covey told me that people sometimes would go into the woods to look for Indian warheads.

One day when I was riding my tricycle in the front yard, I got close to the edge of the hill, where it sloped downward. I went tumbling down the mountain, and I was taken by ambulance to a hospital in a nearby town. I broke both of my collarbones, and my grandparents helped take care of me so my mother could keep working.

One day before I started school, I got into trouble with my grandparents. One of their rules was that I never bothered my grandfather when he was in the living room by himself. I made a mistake once of trying to see my grandfather without permission. My grandmother quickly grabbed me by my arm and dragged me out of the room, holding a yardstick in her other hand. After she punished me, I learned never to bother my grandfather again.

Once I reached school age, my mother moved into

an old two-story house on Wheeling Island. The island was the second-largest populated inland island in the country. It lay between the states of Ohio and West Virginia. Our apartment was on the first floor and beside a bar whose owner was our property owner.

From the first grade through the third grade, my childhood was healthy for a young boy without a father. Until I was eight years old, I had a normal relationship with my mother. I was happy and outgoing. I even had a girlfriend who lived in a house near where I lived.

I can remember that in third grade, I received an award from a teacher for giving the most oral book reports in front of her class. I loved speaking in front of everyone.

After school, my friends and I would play together outside on the sidewalk. We never worried about street violence or being abducted by strangers. In those days, there were no shopping malls, internet, or cable television.

However, everything changed after I completed the third grade. My mother decided to make me repeat the year. The teachers and principal tried to convince my mother that my class grades were not low enough to justify holding me back.

My mother did not take their advice, so she made me repeat third grade. I tried to tell her that I did not want to be held back because I would not be around my friends. Mother would not tell me why she held me back. Something happened to my mother that spring that remained a mystery throughout my life.

By the end of 1960, my happy childhood began to come to an end.

Before that summer, my mother cared for me as any mother would. Around the time my mother made me repeat third grade, her attitude towards me changed, and she also stopped going to the small Methodist church a few blocks from our home.

My mother's personality changed, and she seemed to become almost two different people. She would seem nice to her family and friends, but it was a different story at home. Mother would often criticize me, even for minor mistakes.

At this point, my mother began to work the afternoon shift. Therefore, I had to walk home from school since I lived only a few blocks away.

When I started third grade again, all my friends were in fourth grade. Around that time, I made the mistake of telling my best friend at school that I did not know how to fight. He went and told other children my secret.

Once other boys knew, the bullying began along with name-calling. Being a tall boy for my age with big ears and not defending myself made the rest of my elementary years unbearable. I went from being an outgoing and friendly boy with a girlfriend to a timid boy.

I would dread recess time outside of school because I would be called names by girls and boys. They called me nicknames such as Sexy Rexy and Marvin or T-Rex. It happened so many times that I would try to keep to myself as much as possible. The bullying would also occur inside the school repeatedly for several years.

One day a boy in class made fun of me as our class was leaving. I tried to control my anger as in the past. I knew I did not know how to fight, so I shoved him through two rows of chairs. The teacher sent me to the principal's office

The principal decided to make me speak to a school counselor. Still, even he could not get me to open and share with him why I shoved the boy into the desks while we were lining up to leave the classroom. I refused to talk about my feelings, even though he tried several times. Then he had me bend over his desk, and he spanked me with a thick wooden paddle. I was grateful that he punished me because it meant that he cared.

After that day, I would sometimes wish my mother cared enough to punish me when I disobeyed. She threatened to beat me with a stick one time, but she had another way to make me obey. Her verbal abuse broke my spirit, and I learned to submit to her will and please her. I found that a verbal beating hurt far worse than a physical one.

Walking home was sometimes terrifying to me because bullies would chase me. The quickest way from the school to my house took me underneath the on-ramp that led onto the Fort Henry Bridge, which went from Wheeling Island to Wheeling, or through the Wheeling Tunnels.

One day after school, several boys followed me

home. That day my mother was home. I made it to the door with several boys on the sidewalk near me.

I asked my mother for help when she opened the door, but she told me to handle it myself and that she could not help me, so she closed the door.

The boys called me names and beat me up, and then they left. I knew my mother would not comfort me, so I walked to my backyard and cried.

This was not the only time it happened. Throughout the rest of elementary school, I was abused physically by other boys from time to time. Afterward, I would spend time in the backyard of the apartment I lived in to cry and be alone.

Even on days when my mother was home in the afternoon, I was never given a hug or told I was loved or offered words of encouragement.

My grandmother would visit me from time to time to watch over me when a friend or relative could drive her. Grandma Covey showed me love and supplied some of the discipline I did not receive from my mother. By this time, my grandfather had passed away.

I spent most of my evenings alone in my bedroom. After school, I spent my free time either playing by myself in the backyard of my home or watching shows on television and listening to music.

The combination of physical and emotional abuse at school and not feeling loved at home caused me to become incredibly sad and lonely.

The one thing throughout my childhood that caused me not to take my life was hope. I would tell myself that no matter how difficult life was, the next day might be better.

I spent most of my childhood on Wheeling Island in an apartment just several feet away from a bar. During the weekday evenings there were not too many problems, but the weekends were entirely different.

When night fell, many men would come to the bar and park along the street where I lived because there was no parking lot for the bar's patrons.

Sometimes neighbors called the police to break up fights that carried into the street. One night I never forgot was when several men who were very drunk came over to my apartment. We lived on the first floor, so I could hear the men shouting and cursing out in the street. Several drunken men started to pound on the front door and yelled that they knew I was alone, and they wanted me to open the door and let them inside.

When I was in school, I heard students talk about a building where men would have sex with boys. As the men pounded on my front door, I instinctively knew that if the men broke in, they would attack me and do terrible things to me.

I could hear a man yelling and saying that he knew I was alone, and he told me to open the door so he and his friends could see me. There was no 911 back then or cell phones, and there was no police station on the island. I hid in a room towards the back, trembling with fear. After several minutes, the men went away, but it was hard to sleep that night.

None of my male cousins or uncles took the time to

show or teach me how to become a man. I had a cousin who knew a lot about cars. He tutored his sons but did not show any interest in me.

I looked to three famous political leaders whom I watched on television often. I admired John and Robert Kennedy and Martin Luther King. I especially admired Bobby Kennedy. When I became a teenager, I bought a full-size poster of Bobby Kennedy and taped it on my bedroom door. I tried to pattern my life after these men. They inspired me to help others and be compassionate regardless of our skin color.

During my elementary years on Wheeling Island, my mother could not afford a car. When I wanted to buy a new song, I had to walk across the suspension bridge because it would take me closer to Wheeling, where the stores were.

In 1856, it was the first suspension bridge of its kind in the world. The metal platform where cars would cross and people would walk on both sides had many small openings. I could look down as I walked and see the Ohio River below. The guard rail was a thick wooden beam that ran the entire span of the bridge. More than a few times, I crossed the bridge to look down into the moving river.

I thought about jumping into the chilly waters below to end my life, because I had extremely low self-esteem. However, whenever life seemed hopeless, I would tell myself not to give up because things might be better the next day.

Because my mother stopped going to the Methodist

church after holding me back in third grade, I forgot some of the Bible's teachings that I had learned early. Before my mother left the church, a Sunday school teacher gave me my first Bible in 1961. It was a King James version.

When I was young, the Bible stories I had heard reminded me that God loved me, after my mother stopped going to church.

During my elementary years, my mother had to walk several miles from our home on Wheeling Island to the Ohio Valley Hospital through all types of weather. One winter day, as she walked across the suspension bridge, she slipped and fell on her back. The metal walkway had ice on it because the deck was open to the elements. Mom told me the accident left her with a dislocated disc in her spine, which caused her pain each day afterward.

Less than a month after I turned eleven I was in school, on Friday, November 22, 1963. The principal made a special announcement to tell everyone that the President of the United States had died.

Shortly afterward, when I got home, I turned on the TV to watch what was happening. I was sad because I had looked at President John F. Kennedy as a model of what a man should be. I spent the weekend watching the news about the assassination on a black and white TV set in our living room.

On February 7, 1964, thousands of teenagers gathered at John F. Kennedy Airport to welcome the Beatles. Two days later, on February 9, 1964, the Beatles appeared live on The Ed Sullivan Show. I was one of the seventy-three million viewers who watched them on a black and white TV. I became a fan of them from then on throughout my life.

I would often escape the harsh realities of my life by listening to rock and roll music on a record player that played vinyl records. The music helped me escape the harsh realities of my life.

One of my favorite groups was the Beatles. I also liked to listen to some of the songs by the Rolling Stones. On June 6, 1965, the song "I Can't Get No Satisfaction" was released. It would become their first number one hit in the United States. The song described how I felt about my life as a teenager.

Growing up – teenage years

When I became a teenager, I started my first job as a newspaper carrier for the Wheeling Intelligencer newspaper. I took over a small paper route because the earlier boy was not doing his job correctly.

The other newspaper carriers only rode past customers' homes. They tossed the newspaper towards the house, not caring where it landed.

I took the time to speak to each of my customers and deliver their papers the way they liked. I put their newspaper inside their screen door for some customers, and for others, I put it inside their mailbox.

Over time, I added new customers and built up my route to becoming the largest on Wheeling Island. I was often a winner in contests the company held and won a trip to see the Pittsburgh Pirates. I had the privilege of watching some of the legends of baseball, such as Roberto Clemente, Willie Stargell, and Bill Mazeroski.

On September 6, 1966, Star Trek first aired on television. I quickly became a fan of the show. In Star Trek, I saw a program where everyone cared for each other regardless of their skin color or physical features.

I could relate to Mr. Spock because of his big ears. I watched how he was able to control his emotions, no matter the circumstance. I became not merely a "Trekkie." I emulated Mr. Spock. I focused on controlling my emotions. This was something that would help me throughout my remaining years in school.

As I became even more introverted, I became fascinated with science fiction and time travel. Sometimes after it was dark, I would sit outside on the few steps that led from the sidewalk to the front door. I would take a flashlight and aim it towards the night sky and flash an S.O.S. signal over and over. I hoped that there might be aliens who would see my distress call and come to take me away to a world like Star Trek, where I would be loved and respected. Of course, no help ever came.

Throughout my childhood I would sometimes look at the one black and white photo of my father and myself when I was a toddler. It reminded me that he had loved me. I wondered why he left my mother and me, but I knew that he loved me.

Until I became a teenager, my mother had her family photos organized in photo albums in chronological order. After I had asked one too many times about my father, my mother tore out all the pictures from the collections and tossed them into a metal cookie tin. I assumed it was so I could not figure out the timeline of the photos.

Before this event, there was a postcard with a color photo of my dad with a friend. On the back, my father wrote that his friend was a sweet guy. The writing showed me that my father was a nice man. At some point afterward, the postcard vanished like my father.

Neither my mother nor any family member would say anything negative about my father or his family. This made me believe that my dad was a good man. I figured that if my dad was drunk or mean, then my mother would have said so. Since my mother was very critical of me, I understood why he might have run away. I wondered if my mother had criticized my dad as much as she did to me. In my heart, I knew he did not leave because of me.

I never felt angry with him for leaving. It would be a half-century before I would realize the truth about my father.

When the time came that I was to go to Wheeling High School, which was in Wheeling, my mother rented an apartment only a block away. We lived on the third floor of an old building that had been a saloon in the late nineteenth century. The property owner was a middle-aged man who ran a shoe store on the first floor. There was no central heating in our apartment, so we often heated our small room using a space heater and flames from the kitchen stove. That part of the town was impoverished. The alley behind our home had a bar.

I had dogs as a pet growing up, and they gave me unconditional love, which my mother never gave me.

My mother would complain daily about her job or other events in her life. She would sometimes include herself in her criticisms by telling me that we were dumb or would never amount to anything.

My years in high school were not much of an improvement from elementary school. While the physical bullying stopped, the emotional abuse continued. I tried to evade other students in the hallways as much as possible. My only real friend was a blond-haired girl who was also an outsider because she was overweight.

I have only one happy memory in my four years of high school. It was a day in a biology class when the teacher called out a plant's name of pussy willow, making my friend and me laugh aloud.

When it came time for lunch, I would take my bagged lunch and leave school. I walked behind it several blocks to an old, abandoned factory beside a set of railroad tracks. I would eat my meal there because it was quiet. I did not have to worry about being ridiculed there by other students.

I often sat on what had once been the end of a loading dock and enjoyed the sounds of silence until it was time to return to school and my next class.

Since many evenings after school I stayed in my apartment alone, I had plenty of time to do my homework. The number of television channels was limited when I was in high school. There were only a handful of networks to watch.

I often watched comedy shows because of the variety, such as the Carol Burnet Show and The Three Stooges, and Laugh-In. I spent many hours watching comedians throughout my childhood. Over time, my personality developed a dry sense of humor that would be used later in life to make customers and coworkers laugh.

I watched hundreds of hours of famous comedians like Tim Conway, Johnathan Winters, and the Three Stooges throughout my childhood. Their humor made life more bearable.

My experience in high school consisted of going to classes and trying to avoid other children between classrooms. I had no social life at all. I did not attend social events like proms. A counselor once tried to talk with me to find out why I was so socially introverted. After several meetings, she grew frustrated with me and told me that even the FBI could not get me to talk.

My mother told me she could not always afford to buy me the right size shoes throughout my youth because shoes that would fit me would cost more. Since I did not always have big enough shoes, my toes did not have enough room to grow naturally. The index toe on both of my feet curved inward because there was not enough room to grow straight.

I was able to finish high school as an average student. I was so unpopular that only one student and one teacher signed my yearbook when I graduated in 1971. When the seniors graduated high school with me, most students had a big graduation party with friends and family. For me, all my mother did was drive me to my aunt's house in the country, where we had cake and ice cream.

Besides myself, Aunt Hazel and my mother, only my aunt from Pittsburgh, Pa., and her son congratulated me. We danced on the patio to an album by the Rolling Stones. My Aunt Dee from Pittsburgh danced with me to "Brown Sugar."

Later in the afternoon, I was goofing off with my cousin, "little Lynn." His mother came over to us and told us to listen to her, or she would punish us. I thought that I wished my Aunt Dee could have been my mother because she cared enough about me to discipline me.

Most high school students, when they graduated, had a vision of what they wanted to do, whether to work or go to college. When I went to an employment agency in town, I took a series of tests. When a staff member asked me what type of job I wanted to work at, I told her I had no idea. She referred me to a counselor to help me with deciding what to do with my life.

Since there was no cost, my mother allowed me to visit my counselor. Paul was friendly, and I began to trust him. I opened to Paul about my childhood and my feelings for the first time in my life.

One day he asked if he could come to my apartment where I still lived with my mother. He said he wanted to speak to her about me. He told my mother he believed it would be best for me to go to a public college.

My mother was reluctant to allow me to live on campus. However, Paul was very persuasive. He explained that I had a co-dependent relationship with my mother that was hindering my emotional growth. He explained that he could get a combination of government funding and a work-study program. That way, I could live on campus through the weekdays, which would not cost us anything. My mother agreed, so I decided to go to West Liberty State College in the fall of 1972.

I knew my mother was controlling, but I had been conditioned since a young child to please my mother and do whatever she wanted. I decided to go to college to see what it would feel like to live independently for the first time. West Liberty State College was a public college in the small town of West Liberty, West Virginia. It was the oldest college in West Virginia.

Finding God – 1971

One day after I had graduated high school, a nurse who worked with my mother told her about a summer camp her church was having for teens and invited me to go to it. To my surprise, my mother allowed me to attend the camp that summer. I found being away from my mother for a few days refreshing. I made friends and became good friends with a younger boy.

Each evening the camp counselor held a big bonfire where kids could share their faith and testimonies. It had been years since I was in a Christian setting.

During these evening sessions, we could become Christian. One night, as I stood in front of the blazing fire, staring at the flames shooting above my face, I heard the counselor ask if anyone wanted to give their life to the Lord.

I started to raise my right hand, but my friend told me to wait and think about what I was doing. He told me that I should not act on emotion but think about becoming a Christian. I chose not to give my heart to Jesus Christ that night.

On my way back to the cabin where I was staying, I crossed an old country road. A car with two men drove next to me, and the driver rolled down his window. The driver asked me what I was doing. I explained that I was at a Christian retreat. The driver told me I should be careful walking a dark lonely road at night alone.

I reached the cabin where I was staying and realized that God had been watching over me and protecting me, because the men could have kidnapped me.

While at the retreat, I became outgoing and happy like I had been before being held back in school a decade earlier.

Before the retreat ended, I met a tall girl with long black hair. She struck up a conversation with me, and I found the attention she gave me exciting.

She was attractive, and as we talked, I told her where I lived. Since we lived near each other, my friend invited me to attend her church, as I mentioned that I did not attend church regularly.

Once I had returned from the retreat, I started to attend the Christian Church to meet the girl I had met. I went by myself because my mother was not interested in going to church.

For the first time in my life, I found myself falling in love. We sat together in church beside each other. While we never kissed, the warmth of her fingers intertwined in mine and sitting close beside her in church stirred up emotions I had never experienced before.

We dated throughout the rest of 1971, going to events around Martins Ferry, Ohio, where my girlfriend lived with her two sisters and parents. I thought she loved me.

However, when 1971 ended, I learned that my girlfriend was just using me to make another boy at church jealous. One day she told me that she no longer wanted to see me.

The pain from being rejected by the first girl I ever loved, coupled with learning she had been using me, almost turned me off to Christianity. I thought to myself, if this is how Christians act, then I don't want to have anything to do with them.

Fortunately, my former girlfriend had a sister at church who saw what happened. She spent time talking to me. She helped me to understand that being a Christian does not make you perfect.

I continued to go to the church. However, I sat in the back to not be near the girl who broke my heart. I went to the service on Sundays in the morning and evening.

On March 5, 1972, I went to the evening church service. That night as I listened to Pastor Jim's message, I started to feel my heart rate increasing as he preached.

When he finished, he had an altar call. When I heard that God loved me just as I am, I felt my heart pounding. I wanted to experience the unconditional love the pastor talked about.

I tried to walk up to the front, but I was afraid of what others would think. I tried to step out into the aisle to go upfront, but my feet would not move. The sister of the girl who had dumped me saw that I wanted to become a Christian. She walked over to where I was sitting.

I told her how I was feeling, and she said to me that it was the Holy Spirit calling me to give my life to Jesus Christ. She said she would go with me, so I slowly walked up to where Pastor Jim stood.

Pastor Jim asked me if I wanted to become a Christian. He led me in what is called a sinner's prayer. That night I accepted Jesus Christ as my Savior.

The church I attended was the denomination known as the Christian Church. They believed that water baptism was part of becoming a Christian. Pastor Jim explained what water baptism meant and asked if I wanted to be baptized.

I said I was ready, so I was given an outfit to wear, and I was baptized fully in water that night. I felt for the first time that I was loved and accepted entirely. It was a love and peace that is hard to put into words.

When I returned home to my apartment, I told my mother that I had become a Christian. I thought that she might be happy for me, but she was critical as usual. Mother would see Christians and find faults to justify why she would not become a born-again Christian.

Since I was now twenty years old, I was assertive enough to continue going to church even though my mother would not.

Before the end of summer in 1972, a very unusual event occurred one day in Sunday school. I was sitting in a Sunday school class for teenagers. It started like every other time. However, after a few minutes, two Martins Ferry police officers entered the room. They asked our teacher if a certain boy was there.

The boy stood up, and the officers asked him to come forward. The officers handcuffed him and explained he was going to jail for selling drugs.

The two officers then led the boy out of the classroom and down the hallway to the front door. We were all in shock, and the girls started to cry. I arose from my seat in the back and followed out of the room to see what was happening.

I rushed down the hallway. When I came to the part of the hall that led to the front door, I could see the officers standing outside with our class members.

I must have been in shock because after seeing the police officers outside, I tried to get to the door and forgot several steps.

I realized fast that I was in midair and that I was falling. I managed to adjust my body so that I was able to land on my feet. Unfortunately, I landed at the bottom of the steps with such force that I collapsed in seconds in extreme pain.

As I waited for an ambulance, a friend of mine from the Bible study told me that the drug bust was fake. He explained that the police and the student they arrested knew it was an act. I learned that the youth pastor staged the arrest to teach us the dangers of using drugs.

Then an ambulance came and took me to a nearby hospital. By then, the pain in my left foot was intense.

The hospital staff contacted my mother, who went to the hospital. The doctor had a cast put on my left foot that went up to just below my knee.

He told me that it would have been better if I had broken my foot or ankle because it would have healed properly. The diagnosis was that I had severely sprained my ankle. The doctor told me that I would never walk or run again without a limp after removing the cast.

For the next couple of months that summer, my mother had to drive me around. She would take me to church and pick me up afterward.

My friends from my Sunday school class signed their names and words of encouragement all over my cast. They told me that they would pray that God would heal my foot each Sunday they met until my foot got better.

When the time came for a doctor to remove my plaster cast, he was amazed because I could walk and run normally. I then realized firsthand that God answers prayers.

I wanted to save my plaster cast; however, my mother threw it away shortly after bringing it home. My mother never really considered my feelings or believed things I had were my own.

Before I started college, I received a letter that our government had drafted me for the Vietnam War. I appealed my case to a draft board in my hometown. I came before the board of men that included a pastor.

I tried to express my belief that I did not believe in

killing. Members of the draft board told me that my feelings were irrelevant since I was not a member of certain religious denominations.

The draft board members ordered me to report to a processing station in Pittsburgh, Pennsylvania. Once I went to the government building in Pittsburgh, I wondered if I would be sent off to the Vietnam Conflict afterward.

A military officer took me to a large room where many other young men were standing in several rows. An officer made us undress to our underwear and line up in rows from one side of the room to another.

Standing there being examined by a man I did not know was very humiliating. After the examination, a psychiatrist interviewed me. After answering a series of questions, the man who examined me declared me not qualified for military service for having flat feet and because I was too shy.

Approaching independence

~

When the time approached for me to start college in the fall of 1972, I told my friends at church. They recommended that I go to a Christian college because they were concerned that secular teachers' teachings might influence me. I explained to my friends that God wanted me to go to a secular college to share my faith in the Lord with non-Christian students.

In August of that year I packed my bags, and my mother drove me to the dorm room on campus, where I would be living. It was a new experience for me, being away from my mother on weekdays.

My mother was unwilling to allow me to stay on campus every day, as most students did, so I went home on the weekends. When I was at home during my college years, my mother would want me to tell her what happened to me the previous week.

After I began to live on campus, I discovered that I could not share my faith with the other guys who lived on the dorm floor that I was staying. I wanted to talk to the other students, but I stayed an introvert.

Because of my shyness, my counselor arranged for me to have a private room. My first year was uneventful. I took the classes that were needed and kept to myself when I was in my dorm room. I wanted to tell other students about my faith, but I just could not speak up.

Growing up as a child, I dreamed of being a detective like Joe Friday from the television series "Dragnet." Unfortunately, the college I attended had no law enforcement program. Therefore, I decided to study to be a secondary teacher.

Not long after I had started college, my counselor believed I needed to experience the part of college life that many men experienced off-campus.

Paul arranged for me one evening to visit a home off-campus. There some college students had a party. I reluctantly went by myself. I did not know the other students there, so I kept to myself.

In the kitchen, I noticed an array of diverse types of liquor. I had never drunk alcohol before, but I decided to try. I took a glass and put a small amount of each liquor in it.

Fortunately, a student came into the kitchen just as I was reaching for the last bottle. He said to me, "Don't touch that; it's rubbing alcohol."

The guys there stared at me in amazement as I drank the glass. God watched over me because I did not get drunk and drove back home without any problems. After that experience, I never drank any form of alcohol again.

When I began my sophomore year, I met a new resident manager for the floor I lived on. He was a Christian who shared his faith. After talking with him, he gave me a gospel tract about being filled with the Holy Spirit. He explained how the Holy Spirit could help me witness to people.

One evening I went to the lounge on our floor when no one was around. I sat at a small table in the room. I laid a copy of the New Testament on the table in front of me. It was called the Living Bible.

I closed my eyes, quietly prayed to God, and asked him to help me share my faith with other students. I told God that I needed his help because I could not do it independently.

I had read about the Book of Acts in the Bible and how the Holy Spirit filled the believers. However, there was no sound of rushing wind for me, and I did not feel any different.

After I prayed, I opened my eyes, and a student was standing in front of me at my table. He said he noticed my Bible lying on the desk and asked if I was one of the Jesus People.

I told him that I was. He then went ahead to ask me questions about the Bible. I talked with him without any fear or nervousness. After several minutes, another boy came into the lounge and came over to where I was sitting.

For seven more evenings, I would just go to the room

and sit at a table, and various other students would stop by, and I would share my faith. One evening a couple of boys began asking questions about the Bible that I had not yet learned the answers to.

That night I silently prayed that God would send me another Christian who knew more about the Bible. Shortly after I prayed, two other students came into the lounge. I had met them a few days before and knew they were Christians. However, they did not believe in witnessing to non-believers and usually kept to themselves.

When I told the boys who were questioning me that my friends were Christians, they asked them to come over to where I was. Buck and Roy came over and helped answer the students' questions that I could not.

I became good friends with Buck and Roy after that night. I discovered that they were part of a bluegrass band in their home. Many nights I would go to their dorm room and listen to them play music. Buck would play the guitar, and Roy would play the banjo. They played a rendition of "Dueling Banjos," just like in the movie *Deliverance*, that sounded like the original movie version.

Once during final exams, we decided to spend all night in the lounge on our floor, helping each other study for our finals. Before the sun rose, the lack of sleep got to us, and we began to act as silly as the Three Stooges.

Although I had been a Christian for over eighteen months, my mother was still skeptical of being a

Christian. She always found faults with other Christians and used that as an excuse not to go to church.

One weekend when I returned home from college, my mother seemed happy, which was unusual. She told me that she had begun watching a television evangelist called Ernest Angely.

One day while she sat watching his program, near the end, Reverend Angely prayed for the sick with his hand stretched outward.

Mom described how his hand came through the screen and touched her forehead. At that moment, she said she felt God heal her of her dislocated disc, and all the pain was gone. She then said she gave her heart to the Lord and became a Christian.

My mother became what is known as a Charismatic Christian. Mother believed like I did that God still performed miracles, and the "Gifts of the Holy Spirit" were still for today. However, most of our relatives grew up as Methodists, and they disagreed with my mother's beliefs.

While I respected the different beliefs of others, my mother did not. She often would criticize other relatives who disagreed with her, so some of our family gatherings after that were not the most pleasant.

Adventures in the Holy Land

In 1974 I began viewing a 700 Club program on TV. The Reverend Pat Robinson was a Charismatic Christian. He believed that God still spoke to people through the Holy Spirit and that God heals today.

In late November, Pat Robinson announced that he would take his first trip to Rome, Italy, and the Holy Land in December. I decided to go with Reverend Robinson to see where the New Testament's events took place. My mother was not happy with my decision because I would have to use my life savings to afford the trip.

My mother raised me to please and obey her and do what she wanted. Still, I discovered that my living on campus helped me to mature emotionally. I told my mother that I had made my mind up and that I would take the trip.

I planned with the 700 Club television network to go on the week-long trip to the Holy Land. A week or so before Christmas in 1974, my mother and aunt drove me to the Pittsburgh International Airport in Pittsburgh, Pennsylvania, sixty miles from my home, the nearest airport to Wheeling, W. Va., where I lived.

The time came when I was to board my plane to John F. Kennedy Airport in New York. I started to move towards the gate to board my plane. My Aunt Hazel told my mother to hug me because she might never see me again because of the Palestinian terrorist activity in Israel at that time.

My mother hugged me, and I boarded my plane. Even forty-seven years later, I remember that day because it was the only time I remember that my mother ever hugged me.

My plane landed safely at the John F. Kennedy Airport. I was amazed at how large the area was. I had never been to an airport or city that was so large.

The airport had six passenger terminals and four runways. An interesting fact about the airport is that four years later, to the day, on December 11, 1978, the largest robbery of cash on American soil took place. Thieves stole an estimated 5 million dollars in cash and $875,000 in jewelry from cargo building 261.

It was not hard to find my tour group because Pat Robertson was famous and I knew where I was supposed to meet him. I joined around fifty other Christian pilgrims from around the country at the gate that led to our plane.

Then, after being cleared through security, we boarded our Boeing 707 airplane. The Boeing 707 took off on our non-stop flight to Rome, Italy. While Pat Robertson and his staff rode in first-class, most of us that came with him sat in coach.

Flying in such a large plane was a new and exciting experience for me. However, my flight over was not pleasant. I had to sit beside an older man who smoked. It would not be until 1990 that the federal government would ban smoking on planes.

Our flight took us north over Greenland's tip and then south over Europe to Italy. We were flying so high that I could not see any of the countries or cities below. After a little over eight hours, our plane landed safely in Rome, Italy.

After we went to our hotel, the staff advised us about drinking the local water. Our tour guide told us that many restaurants used wine in place of water in their recipes.

Our tour group stayed together while we visited the popular tourist attractions. When we toured the Flavian Amphitheater, I found it amusing to see an ice cream stand in the same place where the Romans once had Christians fed to the lions.

The Colosseum was finished in 72 AD and had four levels. I learned that the lowest level was for members of the Roman Imperial Court and the emperor. The wealthy families of Rome would sit on the second level. The general population could watch events from the top two stories. It is also the largest amphitheater ever built.

Being able to see the famous Trevi Fountain in Rome

at night was beautiful. The water in the fountain swirled around various stone figures and artificial rocks. It flowed into an expansive basin filled with coins.

We visited the various attractions that tourists usually see. While the statues and beautiful paintings were impressive, the catacombs underneath Rome were my favorite sight to see. I was fascinated by visiting the many tombs built on both sides of the underground walls where our tour traveled. Some areas had beautiful Christian paintings made on the wall above where some of the Christians were buried.

After several days, our tour group boarded our plane for the Holy Land on December 21, 1974. The trip took about three hours and our plane began its descent to land at the Ben Gurion airport. I was surprised to hear the intercom play the Jewish song Hava Nagila throughout the aircraft on speakers. I did not understand the words, but it was very upbeat. At the very moment our plane touched down at the airport, I looked out the window by my seat and saw a sight I never forgot.

Just a few feet from our plane were military jeeps staffed by Israeli security forces. On my right side of the aircraft, I saw one soldier driving. At the same time, another stood using a submachine gun, and they escorted us until we had safely disembarked.

We were fortunate to arrive that day because of what happened on December 20. The day before our arrival, members of the Palestinian Liberation Organization planted a bomb inside a paint can outside a coffee house in Zion Square in Jerusalem. Two Israeli police officers saw the weapon and put it in their police car seconds before it exploded. Fortunately, only a dozen people were slightly injured when the explosive went off.

Pat Robertson had come to the Holy Land partly to complete business deals to run a Christian Broadcasting station in Israel. He arranged for our tour group to use a tour bus run by an Arab company instead of an Israeli company. That was because Palestinian terrorists would often attack tour buses operated by Israeli companies.

We made the thirty-five-mile trip to our hotel, which was on top of the Mount of Olives. Looking at Jerusalem from our hotel was breathtaking. After we had settled in, I became friends with the tour guide. He explained that anyone like me could take a trip to the Holy Land for free. All one had to do was organize a trip and find at least a dozen people to join, then you could go for free because you would be the host.

I also became friends with a couple who had been to Israel several times before. They told me that they knew their way around Jerusalem and could show me sights and things most tourists miss.

That news awakened the "Indiana Jones" inside of me. Growing up, I enjoyed exploring places like wooded areas in the country. My new friends would soon lead me to some unusual experiences during our stay in the Holy Land.

Each morning our group would have breakfast in the dining room of our hotel. Before starting our tour, Pat Robertson would say a prayer for our safety because, during that time, there was a conflict between the Israeli people and the Palestinian people.

We could look out of our rooms and see Jerusalem, the Wailing Wall, and the Dome of the Rock. Just looking at the historical sites made the Bible real to me. Our tour guide had each day planned out for us in detail.

Unfortunately, I could only afford a small 110 mm camera. Our guide recommended purchasing photos of all the attractions in a slide projector format on the tour bus. It seemed like a great idea at the time to me. However, years later, slide projectors became obsolete.

One day we traveled seventy miles to visit the Sea of Galilee, the lowest freshwater lake globally. It was here that Jesus did several miracles, such as walking on water, calming the storm, and feeding the five thousand with only five loaves of bread and two fish.

We had more freedom to look around on our own that day. While I was at the Sea of Galilee, I saw something floating on the water's edge. Being curious, I left our group and went to see what the mysterious object was.

To my amazement, it was a piece of an old green fishing net. I wondered if it might have been a section of the fishing net that the disciples used to go fishing there. The tour guide allowed me to take it with me as a souvenir, and I imagined that it might be part of a fishing net the twelve disciples used.

I was able to do some exploring away from our group several times. One of our stops was at the Dead Sea. The tour bus stopped some distance away from the shore on the western side. We could wade out into the sea because it is impossible to drown because of the high mineral salt concentration.

I learned that I was standing on the lowest point on earth that has air. It is around 1,400 feet below sea level. We learned that asphalt blocks or pebbles often come up to the surface from openings in the bottom of the sea.

In ancient times the bitumen was taken by the Egyptians to use for their mummification process. Many people around the world use soap and face masks made from the mud from the Dead Sea. Later, in 2018, I discovered that using a bar of Dead Sea soap cleared up my psoriasis.

Our tour guide allowed us to walk across the shore and go out into the water. I rolled up my pants legs, and then I took off my shoes and socks and left them at the water's edge. The water was warm and felt greasy.

I waded as far out as I could, some distance from the rest of my group. The sand beneath my feet was warm and soft, and I enjoyed the feeling. There were no fish. No living thing except bacteria can live there.

Because I was tall, I was able to walk out farther than the others in the distance. After a while, I heard the guide tell us that it was time to return to the shore to go to our next sight.

Unfortunately, I was quite a distance from the beach. Being tall and curious, I had wandered away from my group and further out into the waters. I saw the other tourists heading towards the bus. I made a mistake and tried to hurry. I did not realize that buried under the lake's sandy bottom were sharp pieces of stones and rocks. In seconds, my left foot sank in the sand and became trapped between two rocks.

In the distance, I could see the other tourists boarding the bus. I tried waving and yelling, but I could not tell if anyone heard me. I pictured in my mind watching the bus leave without me, leaving me stuck in the Dead Sea. After several minutes I was able to free my foot, but in doing so, I could feel the sharp pain where the rocks had scraped my foot.

I made it to shore and gathered my socks and shoes. Fortunately, my group members told the bus driver of my situation, so he waited for me. I was quite the sight, hobbling onto the bus with my left foot covered in blood. Our tour guide had a first aid kit and bandaged my wounds.

On Sunday morning, December 22, 1974, I learned

that prayer could save your life. In the morning, our group gathered in the dining area of our hotel for breakfast. Because there were several tour groups in our hotel, they had a schedule for each group to leave each morning. When it was our time to go, Reverend Pat Robertson decided we should have a time of prayer. Therefore, another bus could go in our place. Unfortunately for that group of pilgrims, they used a tour bus run by an Israeli company.

The next tour bus started down the road from the top of the Mount of Olives that led into Jerusalem's city when Palestinian terrorists attacked. They threw grenades at the bus. The explosion ripped open a part of the bus's side, seriously injuring a teenager from Jacksonville, Florida. An Arab passenger was also injured.

There was much confusion at first. Israeli soldiers delayed our departure until they could secure the area and capture the terrorists. News of the attack quickly spread around the world through the major networks.

There was no internet, cable television, or cell phones, so I had to use a phone in the hotel to call home collect. My mother and her relatives were genuinely concerned because of the television news reports not reporting any names.

I talked to my mother and Aunt Hazel and told them what happened. I explained that I was safe and would take a tour later in the day. My relatives were happy to hear from me and to know I was okay.

More places to visit

~

Once the Israeli security forces had secured the road leading from our hotel down the Mount of Olives, we left to see more historical sites. I was surprised and disappointed that many famous places were turned into shrines or churches by the Catholic church hundreds of years ago.

Our trip took us through the Via Dolorosa. We walked through the fourteen stations that started where Pontius Pilot condemned Jesus to death. We ended up at the Church of the Holy Sepulcher in the Old City of Jerusalem. I was at the church where what I saw made the Bible real to me. I was fascinated to learn about the history of the church.

The church was declared sacred in 335 AD. However, the Persians set it on fire in 614. Several years later, the abbot Modestus restored the church. In 1009 AD, the church was destroyed again and later rebuilt by the Crusaders. Much of the Church of the

Holy Sepulcher now standing dates to 1610.

Just inside the entrance was a stairway that led up to the Calvary site known as Golgotha. Archaeologists have found out the church stands on a Jewish cemetery site that dates to Jesus's time. I made my way to what is called the Altar of the Crucifixion.

Scholars often debate the exact location of many of the Biblical sites in Israel. Although church leaders had covered the area with an altar and many beautiful objects made of precious metals, I spotted something unexpected. I looked down at the altar's right side and was surprised to see what appeared to be a small section of the actual hill. What I saw next, I have never forgotten.

I saw three round holes in the ground, and to the right of the center hole, I saw a thin fissure where the area appeared to have cracked open. Then I remembered that in Matthew's Gospel, Chapter 27, the Apostle Matthew wrote that an earthquake happened when Jesus died and that saints that were dead rose from the grave.

I then realized that I was standing right in front of the spot where the Roman soldiers crucified Jesus. My faith was deepened that day. It was one thing to read about the event in the Bible, but standing in the place made the Bible more real and deepened my faith.

I formed a theory that day about how the dead saints rose from the dead after Jesus was crucified. The Gospels record that when a Roman soldier pierced the side of Jesus when he was on the cross, blood and water flowed out.

Since the blood of Jesus Christ is powerful, I theorized that when his blood dripped or flowed down, it landed on the ground between him and the thief beside him. As the Messiah's blood flowed onto the dirt ground, it was so powerful that it dissolved the earth and continued to flow through the soil. When his blood landed on the dead saints buried deep below, it caused them to come to life again.

Protestants tend to believe the "Garden Tomb" to be the burial place of Jesus. I discovered later that many scholars believe that the actual tomb where Joseph of Arimathea buried Jesus after the crucifixion is inside the Holy Sepulcher's Church.

The shrine that encases the tomb of the Messiah is called the Aedicula. While at the "Garden Tomb" site, we could look inside to see that it was empty.

However, at the Aedicula is where the Catholic Church believes is the actual burial space of Jesus. They sealed the tomb in 1555 AD with a massive marble slab. Church officials did that to keep pilgrims from taking pieces of the grave with them as souvenirs. We were not able to see inside that tomb of Jesus to know that it was empty.

However, on October 26, 2016, thirty researchers were given sixty hours to open the tomb of Jesus and examine it. They found the burial site of Jesus to be empty, of course. Archeologists have found other graves in the area, which proves the area near the Crucifixion location was a Jewish cemetery that dates to Jesus's time.

The following day after breakfast, Pat Robertson took our tour group inside Jerusalem. I experienced an event "Indiana Jones" reminded me of years later when the movie came out. We entered through the Dung Gate and could walk around the vast plaza connected to the "Wailing Wall," also known as the Western Wall. I learned that when the Romans destroyed the Second Temple and much of Jerusalem in 70 AD, they left the Western Wall intact.

We could go to the wall and pray with the other pilgrims and Jews. Many people take a small piece of paper, write their prayer requests, and place it inside the wall's small openings.

Twice a year, the Rabbis oversee the wall and collect the prayer requests to make room for more. Then they take the old pieces of paper and bury them on Jerusalem's Mount of Olives, where we stayed overnight.

While our tour group could roam around the plaza, my two friends who had been there several times told me to go with them to where a tall man was talking. He was a Jewish Christian who was famous during the 1970s. We walked over to where he was standing on a small platform.

He was speaking to a group of pilgrims who were members of his group to the Holy Land. We found his speaking remarkably interesting. What happened next was unforgettable. When he had finished speaking, he invited all of us who listened to him to go with him for a special tour that most tourists could not see.

What I saw there I would never forget. The long walk to the left of the Wailing Wall was thirty-nine meters away from the Dome of the Rock, an Islamic shrine built around 692 CE. The Muslims believe that the area is where the prophet Muhammad was taken by the angel Gabriel to heaven. The Jews believe that the rock is the spot where Abraham prepared to sacrifice his son Isaac.

Many Jews and Christians believe that the Dome is where Herod's Temple stood at Jesus's time. However, other scholars believe the actual Temple site is further away from the City of David.

We followed the speaker and his group after he finished speaking. Israeli soldiers allowed me and my friends to enter an entrance to a building where most tourists were not allowed. They did so because we were with the tour group of a famous Jewish Christian.

Once inside, we could not take any photos, so no one could prove anything they might try to share after leaving. We stood inside a narrow walkway that stretched as far as the eye could see in both directions. Several feet in front of me was a tall steel fence that went from the ground up to the ceiling above me. I noticed that armed Israeli security guards patrolled the area.

Off in the distance, archaeologists could be seen working. They were working on uncovering a section of Jerusalem believed to have existed at the time of Jesus. The men who were working there appeared tiny to me. In the distance was an area suspected to be the actual site of where Herod's Temple had once stood.

I saw what appeared to be a long bridge-like structure that led to a spot where some type of architecture had once stood. I wondered if I was looking at a part of the actual Jerusalem that existed at the time of Jesus. Years later, I watched a video taken by a famous television minister. I learned that some distance to the left from where I was that day is where some scholars believe the lost Ark of the Covenant lies buried. If that is true, that might explain some unique experiences I was to have later in life.

Another part of our tour was to visit the Jordan River. It is the lowest river in the world. Christians consider the Jordan River the third most holy site in the Holy Land because John baptized Jesus there and it is where his ministry began.

A minister baptized several of our tour group there. Being adventurous, I discovered an empty tall wine bottle floating in the water near the shore. I used it to gather some water from the Jordan River to keep as a souvenir.

After our tour had ended on Christmas Eve evening, we went to our hotel for the night. Because of Bethlehem's danger of terrorist attacks that night, our tour group could not go there that evening.

My two friends told me that they knew how to get into Bethlehem that night. Being curious, I accepted their offer to go there with them. We went to the front desk and asked for our passports. The desk clerk told us that they had locked our documents in a safe, and the hotel would not give them to us. My two friends said to me that they could hire a taxi to take us to Bethlehem, and they knew how to get inside the city of Bethlehem.

They contacted a taxi driver, and we decided to leave the hotel. The trip from Jerusalem to Bethlehem took about thirty minutes. Our driver stopped before entering the city because he believed it to be too dangerous.

We left the car and began to walk the rest of the way. What we were doing was so exciting, I never thought about what could happen to us if the security guards had caught us without our passports.

Israeli soldiers had set up roadblocks in the streets leading into the town that evening. Only tourists with special passes were being allowed into the city to visit the birthplace of the Messiah. Since my friends had been there several times before, they led me past the checkpoints. There were thousands of pilgrims from many countries walking around the city that night. The town is inside the West Bank, and the Kingdom of Jordan supplies security at Manger Square.

I did not have a ticket to enter Saint Catherine's Church in Manger Square, so I joined many other pilgrims outside. There was a large screen set up on the front of the church, and at midnight, we watched the Pope give his midnight mass from Rome live.

Then we went to the Church of the Nativity. It was built in 326 CE by the Roman Emperor Constantine on the site believed to be where Jesus Christ was born. I had to duck to enter the door that led into the church. Catholic priests had built the first entrance much more extensively. I learned that the Crusaders made the opening smaller to prevent future attackers from riding horses into the church.

After entering, I descended a flight of stairs where I came to the Grotto of the Nativity.

At last, I had reached the spot where Jesus Christ was born. An elegant shrine covered the location of the manager. A fourteen-pointed silver star on top of a marble floor marked the manger scene. To me, the area looked like a fireplace one would see inside the Taj Mahal.

Around the manger scene was the Altar of the Adoration of the Magi. It had paintings of the three wise men, Caspar, Balthazar, and Melchior.

In 614 CE, the Persians attacked Palestine. They spared the church and the cave because they saw the magi's depictions in their native costumes.

After my friends and I had visited the manger's site, we made our way through the town and were able to find a taxi to take us back to our hotel. I was sleepy in the morning as I had to get up early for our last day of touring.

On our last day, we visited Bethlehem's town, where I had been the night before. We then saw the upper room, where he had his last supper with his disciples and where the Holy Spirit first came to the disciples.

The upper room was a large dining hall on the

second floor of a building south of the Zion Gate. There is no table there, as is often associated with paintings about the last supper of Jesus. Archaeologists have found pieces of plaster inside the building with Greek writing. One report had the word Jesus written on it.

We then went to the Chapel of the Ascension, the site where tradition holds that Jesus went up into heaven. The chapel was built on the Mount of Olives, close to our hotel. Inside was a slab of stone that is said to hold the imprint of Jesus's right foot. The chapel initially did not have a ceiling. Our tour guide explained that after the Muslims captured Jerusalem, they built a dome over the chapel. It has remained under Islamic control to this day.

The following day we arose early to have our last breakfast in our hotel. We then boarded our bus with Pat Robertson to head to the Ben Gurion International Airport for our flight back home.

When our plane began to take off, Israeli soldiers armed with machine guns mounted on top of their jeeps escorted us. While our flight left without incident, Pat Robertson's son stayed behind. As his plane took off the following day, Palestinian terrorists shot at the airplane with a spray of bullets from machine guns. Fortunately, the terrorist attack did not injure anyone on board.

After returning to Wheeling, W. VA, I prepared to go back to college in the fall. My trip had deepened my faith as a Christian. I had a brown bag that held my souvenirs from my pilgrimage. Unfortunately, not long after my return, my mother threw away the fishing net section from the Sea of Galilee. My mother never respected my wishes since I lived with her. Nothing that I considered valuable meant anything to her.

Forty-five years later, only one souvenir is still around, which is a bracelet that I bought my mother while in Israel. It holds four hand-carved flowers made from the ivory tusk of an elephant from Africa. The following year, in 1975, countries around the world banned international trade in Asian elephant ivory.

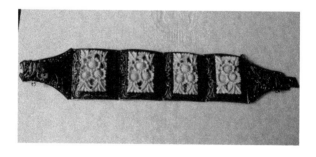

Getting more involved
with the Church

~

After my return from the Holy Land, I began to become acquainted with what is known as the Charismatic movement.

I lived about sixty miles from Pittsburgh, Pennsylvania, the home of evangelist Kathryn Kuhlman. She was well known for her healing ministry. One day I decided to go on a chartered bus that was going from Wheeling to see her. We stopped at the historic Carnegie Hall in downtown Pittsburgh. Ms. Kuhlman was the most famous woman evangelist in the world at that time. Every Friday evening, she would hold a healing service.

When our bus arrived, the church was already almost filled. It looked like the ushers would have to turn us away. Still, at the last moment, a man who was part of the evangelist's team came and said there were some seats on the stage directly behind where Ms. Kuhlman would be preaching.

Kathryn Kuhlman introduced herself to the audience after we had sung some hymns. I had seen her on her television program, but to see her in person was quite different.

She appeared in a flowing white chiffon gown with long sleeves, which made her look like an angel, combined with her dark, curly hair. Both Protestants and Catholics filled the church. Pope Paul VI has given her his blessing.

I sat several rows behind where she was ministering. She made it clear in each of her services that not she but Jesus Christ was the healer. After her message, Ms. Kuhlman started her healing ministry.

She would begin by telling members of the audience that God was healing them of various illnesses. Near the end of her church service, Ms. Kuhlman turned around to face those of us on the stage.

She began to walk past each row of believers slowly. Kathryn did not touch anyone. However, as she came by each row of chairs, I saw some people gradually slump into their chairs. I had heard about people being overwhelmed while in the presence of the Holy Spirit. However, I had never seen it before except on her television programs. As she passed by my row, I firmly gripped the seat in front of me as I was afraid to experience what I saw happening to others near me.

People in the service testified that God had healed them. Ms. Kuhlman told everyone that it was the Lord who did the healing. She had a few of the people in the audience come onto the stage. Then she allowed them to talk about how the Lord had healed them.

College life

As I began my next college semester, I met two young Christian girls at an off-campus ministry. It was a weekly meeting for Christian students to get together to talk and have fun. A young married couple hosted the meetings at their home in the small town of West Liberty. They were members of a Christian organization known as Campus Crusade for Christ.

I went to the weekly meetings off-campus to meet other Christians and became friends with two young girls as we found out that we had similar faiths. Donna, Janet, and I were what were known as Charismatic Christians. Most of the other Christians at my college were evangelical. The three of us did not fit in because we believed that God still healed today and that the Gifts of the Holy Spirit still existed.

As the weeks went by, I developed an interest in Donna, who was short with blond hair and played in the college band. One weekend when I was home with my mother, the college band came by our home as they marched in a parade. It took time, but I finally managed the courage to share my feelings with Donna. She told me that she came from a wealthy family and that she already had a boyfriend. However, we remained good friends.

When I was on campus in 1975 and 1976, I would meet Donna and Janet several evenings each week. There was an interfaith chapel on the campus, and one evening, we discovered the door to be unlocked. We went inside and sat down in a pew close to the beautiful stained-glass windows on both sides.

Donna and Janet sat on opposite sides beside me, and then we would hold hands. We then spent time quietly praying aloud, usually all at the same time. What I felt was not a romantic feeling as we prayed and worshiped God. I felt like I had two sisters. We became close friends.

Every evening, we would meet in the evening near the chapel, and we would find the door open, so we went inside to spend time praying together. Our friendship deepened throughout my junior year of 1975. Each evening after I spent time praying with Donna and Janet, I would walk them back to their dorm, which was on the opposite side of the campus from where I lived.

Our college separated the boys and the girls, so their dorms were on opposite ends. Naturally, female students found ways to sneak into the male dorms and vice versa.

One evening in spring, when the weather was warm, the three of us stopped at a bench made of concrete. It was between the college library and the girls' dorms near the main entrance.

We decided to sit down and spend some more time praying. Donna and Janet sat beside me on opposite ends. We held hands, bowed our heads, and began to pray aloud softly.

After a few minutes of praying with my eyes closed, I could see a bright light coming towards me. I assumed it was just a car coming into the campus. Seconds later,

I felt the presence of someone standing in front of me. I was afraid to open my eyes to look because I thought it must be a student wondering why the three of us were sitting there praying. When we stopped praying and opened our eyes, both of my friends had tears in their eyes.

They asked me if I saw anything while we were praying. I told my girlfriends that I could see a bright light with my eyes closed, and I felt someone in front of me. Then they both told me what happened to them. Both girls told me they saw Jesus walk up to them. They described him as dressed all in white with long black hair.

Then they explained how Jesus stretched out his hands. He placed one hand on each of them, and then he bent down and kissed me on the forehead. Seconds later, they said Jesus was gone. I was aware that some Christians believe God sends people visions.

Donna and Janet went into their dorm, and I walked back to my dorm that night, pondering the meaning of what had just happened. I wondered if the bright light I saw and the presence of someone standing in front of me as I was praying could have been Jesus Christ, as my friends had described.

One of my required courses in secondary education in 1975 was a religion course. Our professor designed his class to expose us to different religions. One day we went to the college chapel to hear the leader and founder of the Hare Krishna movement in West Virginia.

Swami Prabhupada spoke to us. Several members of his commune accompanied the spiritual leader. They all had shaved heads, wore long white gowns, and had tambourines, which they used when singing their chants.

The swami spoke to us about the Hare Krishna faith. He was the founder of the Hare Krishna movement. I learned in class that his views on religion were quite different than mine, so I was curious to hear what he believed.

The guru explained that he believed that God was Krishna and that their God had a physical form. He also shared that his faith was Hinduism and that he believed in reincarnation and not eating meat. He spoke about love and peace. However, his demeanor changed quickly when a member of our class asked him a question.

One of the students from our class asked the swami what they would do if parents tried to take their children from their commune. He said they would use pitchforks and force to stop them. I had seen news reports months before that some parents believed that their children were brainwashed by the swami. After hearing Swami Prabhupada, I was convinced that he was a cult leader.

Another semester in college

In the summer of 1975, most students went home to their families. I could live on campus because I worked during the summer at the college library. I still went back to live with my mother on most weekends. The summer months seemed to go by quickly.

When I started the fall semester, I discovered my friendship with Donna and Janet had changed. Upon our first meeting, I could tell Janet was upset. She informed both of us that she had to drop out of college. Janet told us that during the summer, she got involved in a church in her hometown. It was a non-denominational charismatic church. Janet went on to describe that the pastor called himself a prophet. He convinced his followers that God spoke to him and told him whom each member should marry.

Tears streamed down her face as she explained that the "prophet" prophesied she was to marry a man in the congregation. Donna and I tried to make her understand that the man was a false prophet, but she decided to drop out of college. When Janet left college, Donna no longer met with me for prayer in the chapel at night, like before.

In my junior year, I met a young man at an off-campus weekly meeting of Christian students. He was not well accepted there because he was of the Mormon faith, and he was blind in his left eye. Throughout my junior year, we became good friends.

We did not talk a lot about the differences in our faith. We respected our different beliefs. In the evenings, we would often meet at a tennis court near our dorm room. I knew he was blind in one eye so that I could have easily won each game. I made it a point to try as often as possible to return the ball on the side where his seeing eye was. Our time together taught me that we should not judge people by how they look.

That year I had to take a math class to meet my teaching requirements. I thought that the statistics class would be easy. I quickly discovered that I could not understand even the basics. I started to flunk the course.

Fortunately, the college offered tutoring help. For the first half of the course, my tutor helped me understand the principles, and I went from an F to a B average. Unfortunately, my tutor had to leave to do student teaching in the middle of my course.

The college officials gave me a tutor who was not as skilled, so by the end of the course, I flunked the class. I learned just how important each person is and how our decisions can affect other's futures.

During my senior year, my program required me to do student teaching. I saw a class in a school in my hometown. Unfortunately, the teacher I studied under had worked for many years and only had negative things to say about teaching. Instead of encouraging me to enter education, he recommended that I get out of the teaching field. The teacher pointed out that it was hard to get a full-time job in West Virginia, especially in secondary education. I also realized that my shyness would be a problem in ever becoming a teacher.

Not long after I began student teaching, the college informed me that I would not graduate because I had failed the statistics class. I would be allowed to graduate with my other classmates. However, all the college would give me was a blank piece of paper, and I would get my degree only if I took the math class after I graduated.

I was very discouraged and thought about my options. At that same time, West Virginia offered a new type of college degree, a Bachelor of Arts degree in life studies. Between having my student teacher discourage me from teaching and taking another class after graduation, I chose to drop out of education.

My mother and several cousins came that spring to see me graduate. I walked onto the stage to receive my diploma on a warm sunny day and said goodbye to my friends.

An unpleasant experience

A few months after graduating from college, I saw the guidance counselor who helped me go to college. We met in a parking lot where Paul invited me to his home some evening. He wanted to find out how I was doing.

A few days later, I drove over to his home one evening. Inside, Paul invited me to sit with him on his couch. I noticed a small glass with alcohol in it to my left. As he began to talk, he offered me a drink. I told him I did not like to drink alcohol after I tried it once in college.

As Paul was talking about his new profession, I could smell alcohol as he spoke. He also had an evil sort of grin on his face that reminded me of the comic tv character "The Joker." Paul said he counseled sex offenders in prisons. As he started to describe what they talked about, he moved closer to me. I could tell that he was drunk, but I trusted him because he was my closest friend.

Then Paul reached over and touched my leg. He began to describe what he wanted to do to me sexually. I tried to reason with him, but it did no good. As Paul tried to force himself on me, I seemed to be frozen in place. I wanted to leave quickly, but Paul was also the first person in my life that I had opened to in counseling, and I did not want to offend him.

After realizing that Paul would not take no for an answer, I felt anger rise inside me. I had let bullies beat me up when I was a kid, but now my self-esteem had grown. I pushed Paul away from me and ran out the front door before he could complete his assault.

When I got home, I told my mother what had happened. Needless to say, she was upset with my friend. When Paul called me the next day, my mother answered the phone. Paul tried to apologize, but my mother told him never to contact me again. I lived with a feeling of guilt about what had happened to me even though I was the victim. Over time I was able to feel better about myself. However, I would never again allow myself to develop a close friendship with a man for the rest of my life.

After graduation, I began to attend a church in my hometown called The House of Prayer. Our church became part of the 700 Club's phone ministry. I decided to become a telephone counselor at their call center. The counseling center gave me a counseling handbook. It had various scripture verses for different problems callers might have.

One night a young man called, and I answered. He

told me that he was an atheist. He rejected the scripture verses I gave him. He said that I could not prove God exists. I tried to think of how I could prove to him that God exists. I was not skilled at memorizing scripture verses, so I decided to tell him my testimony.

I told him about my childhood and life experiences and what being a Christian meant to me. Before he hung up, he said to me that he was not ready to become a Christian. However, he told me that he did believe there was a God after listening to my testimony.

Church – 1979-80

~

In 1979 my mother became interested in a small church near Pittsburgh, Pennsylvania. The pastor of the church was a woman. Her first name was Velma, and she was Charismatic. My mother and I would drive over half an hour on Sundays to attend the church services.

Velma taught the congregation that each of us could pray for the sick and see the Lord heal people. She believed that miracles in prayer were not just for famous evangelists like Earnest Angely or Kathryn Kuhlman, but all Christians.

Throughout 1979 and 1980, I started to study the Bible through a correspondence course she offered. Even though I was still introverted, I thought that I could become a minister.

While attending the services, another church member introduced me to a young woman. Although we lived in towns over thirty miles apart, I decided to ask Debbie out on a date. We had similar interests, and when we were apart, we would write to each other. Computers with the internet and cell phones only existed then in science fiction shows like Star Trek.

After several months of dating, we found ourselves falling in love. I proposed to my girlfriend, and she said she would marry me. Until this point, my mother was supportive of my love interest. Even though I was independent, my mother still controlled me emotionally to tell her about my personal life.

Unfortunately, when we talked about married life, I discovered that Debbie was comfortable charging items and debt. On one of our dates, she told me that she had a dream. Debbie said to me that she saw a baby crib with several babies in her dream. She believed that God showed her that we were to have several children.

I found the fact that my fiancée liked to charge things and wanted children overwhelming. Although I was out of college, I only had a job at a local restaurant. I was afraid that I could not afford to get married.

When I told my mother about my concerns, she said that I should not get married. My mother had raised me in a co-dependent relationship. Even as a young boy, I always tried to please my mother.

When I decided to not leave my mother and start a new life, I decided to break off my engagement. Debbie was brokenhearted, as was I but, I was not strong enough emotionally to leave my mother.

In 1980 I was hired by a catalog showroom called Service Merchandise. It was a full-time job in a shopping mall in a small town in Saint Clairsville, Ohio. I spent most of my time from 1980 until 1989 working forty hours a week and living at home with my mother. She never encouraged me to move out on my own.

Running

On the last weekend of May in 1980, I decided to try out for a race held each year in my hometown. I was a fast walker but knew that I was not ready for such a race. However, I decided to try it. That Saturday, runners from around the world had arrived. The race was about half the distance of the Boston marathon.

It started in town and went through the city of Wheeling. The last part was going up Wheeling Hill, leading back into town to the finish line.

As the race began, the elite runners quickly faded into the distance. By the time I had reached Wheeling Hill, I was at the end of the pack. I saw senior citizens running past me. I was dehydrated and exhausted by then. However, I experienced something then I never had before. People lined up along both sides of the streets.

Most runners had long since passed by me. However, I saw the onlookers clapping and cheering for those of us who were going by. They treated me like I was a champion, which was something I never experienced before.

By the time I reached the bottom of the tall hill, a security truck had offered to ride me to the finish line. I was exhausted, but I felt so encouraged by the spectators, I turned down their offer.

As I reached the top and began going down the hill, I was in pain and thirsty. By the time I finally made it to the finish line, the crowds were already gone. A few people were still around to watch the last runners finish.

After I crossed the finish line, I collapsed onto the pavement. The medical team there rushed me to the hospital where my mother worked. After they treated me, I was able to walk home as I lived nearby. The following day, my hometown newspaper listed me as one of the runners whom ambulances had to take to the hospital.

I always remembered the race because, for the first time in my life, I felt important, and people treated me like I was a winner even though I lost.

Seven hours with Jesus

During the spring of 1980, the church pastor near Pittsburgh, Pennsylvania, passed away. She contracted a disease during a mission trip and never recovered. Her associate pastor became the lead pastor and renamed the church Greater Works Outreach.

That summer, the church sponsored a weekend Bible conference held at the University of Pittsburgh. I stayed the weekend on campus because the students were away for the summer. Each of the three days was spent attending various lessons or sermons taught by the local pastor or a visiting evangelist.

After the Saturday evening meeting was over, I went back to my dorm room. Since my room was several floors up, I decided to take an elevator. While waiting for the elevator, I met two women and a visiting African American minister. On our way up to our rooms, he suggested that we stop at a lounge on our floor.

When we went inside, the minister invited us to sing some worship songs. While we were singing, I looked to my left and saw people walking in the hallway, heading for their dorm rooms to get ready for bed. After a few minutes, the minister spoke to me. He looked at me and told me that God had spoken to him and that he was supposed to pray for me.

I walked over and stood in front of him. The two women stood behind me in case I was "Slain in the Spirit." That is a term used to describe people who slowly fall to the floor when they feel the presence of God. When he prayed for me, he touched my forehead with his hand. In seconds I found myself lying on my back on the floor of the carpeted lounge. While I was lying on my back with my eyes closed, I raised my hands straight up and started to repeat the words, I love you, Jesus, over and over.

At that moment, I had my eyes closed; however, I felt myself standing upright. I had read reports before about people who died, gone to heaven, and then returned. However, I knew I was still alive. What I was now experiencing felt natural to me.

I could see that I was standing on a floor that appeared to be surrounded by clouds on every side. Then I noticed a tall man standing beside me on my right side. He had on a long white robe and dark black hair. I did not see his face, but I knew it was the Lord. I felt a peace and love that was unlike anything I had ever experienced.

Then scenes or memories from my past began to

appear a few feet in front of me. It was like watching them in black and white on a large screen. Each time a painful memory or experience appeared, it felt like the Lord touched it with his hand. That memory was still there but without any negative feelings attached to it. Time had no meaning to me while this was happening. It seemed like the Lord was taking me back through my past and healing the painful memories that had turned me from an outgoing child to an introverted adult. The longer my experience went on, the more joy and peace and love I felt.

I finally opened my eyes and looked up from the floor where I lay. The minister was standing nearby, and two women sat in a chair to my left. They told me that it was morning already. They helped me to stand up. I looked to my left, and in the hallway I saw the same people I noticed after I first entered the lounge. They looked at us strangely because it was now morning, and they were getting ready for breakfast.

The minister told me that I had lain on my back with my hands straight up softly, worshiping God for around seven hours, saying, Jesus, I love you, over and over. He told me that he knew God was touching me, so he stayed with me the whole night. I then went to get a shower and get ready for breakfast. I felt so happy and free emotionally. While I showered, I found myself singing praise songs out loud. I thought that this must be what I would have felt if my dad had raised me. I no longer felt shy or sad.

At the elevator, I met the evangelist and the two

women who had been with me overnight. While we were going down to the main floor, the evangelist taught us a valuable lesson. He said that people may make us doubt our beliefs, but they cannot make us examine something we experienced. I went home after the meetings were over that day, but I felt like a new person. When I got home, my mother could tell that I had experienced something special. I explained to her what had happened to me. She did not seem to doubt my experience. I assumed that was because growing up, I noticed that she bought magazines about the supernatural.

The following Sunday, after I returned home, I went to the church pastor we attended. I asked him if I could speak to the congregation. He allowed me to talk because he could tell something had happened to me.

Usually, I would be quiet and sit towards the back of the church. That Sunday, I stood in front of the congregation. I told them what had happened to me at the Bible conference. For the following few months, I was outgoing and confident.

I continued to study for the ministry through a Bible correspondence course. The course was from the church in Pittsburgh, Pennsylvania, I used to attend. It moved to Monroeville, Pennsylvania.

In 1981 I noticed that my personality began to revert to being more introverted. I reasoned that the everyday struggles of life were the reason. On the twenty-third day of August 1981, I received a Certificate of License as a minister of the whole gospel of Jesus Christ. It was signed by the two lead pastors of Greater Works Outreach in Monroeville. Pennsylvania. Unfortunately, by this time, I was no longer the outgoing and self-confident man I was a year earlier.

Bible studies with an exorcist

∼

In 1983 a friend at church told me about an unusual Bible study led by a real exorcist. Having a curious nature, I decided to go to a meeting. The weekly meeting was at the home of the exorcist, in a small town called Shadyside, Ohio, near the West Virginia border.

I went to the meeting in the evening that was led by an older woman minister called Irene. I went down to her basement, where she held her Bible study. Most of the people there were women. Irene taught the Bible, but she also talked with us about exorcism.

I found the first meeting fascinating, so I started to go each week. The following week a woman asked Irene why she did not have exorcisms at our meetings. Irene explained that she had tried an exorcism during a Bible study when she first began doing exorcisms. Unfortunately, not everyone there had spent time praying before the exorcism.

When Irene cast out the demon from the person she was praying for, the devil entered another person there. The man became violent, and several other people held him long enough for Irene to do an exorcism.

I learned that anyone trying to do exorcisms must pray a lot and confess any hidden sins first. At one meeting, Irene told us that ministers from churches in surrounding cities knew about her. When they could not help someone through counseling, they would send that person to her for an exorcism. She told us about one exorcism involving a boy.

She learned that his family played with a Ouija board game they bought in a toy store. She said to him that the game would open the players up to being attacked by real demons. Then she instructed him to go home and destroy the board game. He returned later to tell Irene what happened.

The young boy told Irene that his parents took the Ouija board and tossed it into a fire in their yard. As the fire started to melt the game, the family said they heard loud demonic screams coming from the fire.

At the end of each Bible study, we would gather in a circle to pray. One week, Irene told us that she saw a vision from God. She described seeing the Apostle Luke, the physician. Irene described him as wearing a white robe with a head mirror on his head.

Then she saw him walk behind each of us. He put one hand on the shoulder of each person until he came to me. Then she said she saw the Apostle Luke put a hand on both of my shoulders and look up to heaven and smile.

The following week as we were in a circle praying, Irene had another vision. This time she told us that she saw Jesus dressed in a bright white robe with long black hair.

Irene described how he walked behind each person and placed a hand on one of their shoulders. Then Irene said she saw Jesus stand behind me. He placed one hand on each of my shoulders, looked to heaven, and smiled. By this time, I wondered why each vision had something extraordinary that applied to me.

As we were praying, Irene had me stand in the middle of the group we prayed with during another Bible study. Irene told us that she saw a large white sheep standing in front of me. Then she said it stood up on its hind legs and put its front paws on my chest.

At this point in my life, I felt like I had failed God. Several years earlier, I had studied to be a minister, but I learned that I did not have the needed self-confidence. I had a difficult time believing the Lord would love me as much as Irene's visions suggested. I never told my mother about the supernatural things that Irene had seen about me.

I was quiet during our Bible studies and rarely spoke even though I had studied the Bible for over a decade. At another meeting during prayer, Irene again asked me to stand in the middle as we prayed. Then she described seeing a scroll rolled up floating inside of me. This time she said it meant that I knew the Word of God inside me, but I needed to let it out and talk.

The visions Irene saw about me seemed genuine, but I still could not bring myself to open up and share what I knew. After my experience in 1980 with the Lord, I was more outgoing and self-confident for a time. However, now I felt like I was back to the person I had been most of my life by this time. I believed it was because I lived with my mother, who always negatively impacted my life.

I enjoyed going to Irene's Bible studies. Over time Irene learned that I still lived with my mother. She tried to find a duplex for us to live in Shadyside, Ohio. Sadly, she made the mistake of talking to my mother about it. Irene thought that my mother could live on one side, and I could live on the other. The idea of my having that type of independence did not go over well with my mother. Even at 31 years old, my mother still was against me living on my own. My mother refused to move and did not want me to go to further meetings. Thus, my time with the exorcist ended.

I spent the next seven years working and taking care of my mother. I was having a co-dependent relationship with my mother that allowed me no time to think about my father or even my wants or needs.

In 1989, something happened that would start a chain of events in motion that would culminate with meeting my father thirty years later.

How "Back To The Future" changed my life

In the fall of 1989, the company I worked for went out of business. For the first time in a decade, I was out of work. I began to think about my future, as well as my past.

For most of my life, I lived with regrets about my past. I thought about what my life could have been if my father had not left. I also often wished I could have made better decisions in the past.

One day I watched an interview on TV with Christopher Lloyd about time travel. He said that while we cannot change the past, we can change the future. I always liked shows about time travel, but I never realized that I could change my future. When I watched the *Back to the Future* movies, I saw "Doc Brown" explain how our decisions can create a new timeline.

When I saw the interview that day, I realized that today's decisions would change my future. I could give up on life and settle for the mundane, as I had, or I could do something daring. I decided to make a meaningful change in my life. I told my mother that I wanted to leave Wheeling, W. Va., and move to Ohio and find a better job. Even though I was thirty-seven years old, I still felt the need to tell my mother. She was retired from her career as a nurse by then.

I was determined about moving, so my mother approved, provided she came along. I started to research jobs and towns in Ohio. I finally decided on Canton, Ohio.

Because of winter coming, I moved to Canton in the early spring of 1990. My mother and I moved into a mobile home a few miles from Canton. Even though I was thirty-eight years old, my mother was unwilling to allow me to move out independently. I did not realize then how my mother had groomed me to be co-dependent from early childhood.

After a few weeks of working temporary jobs, the manager of a catalog showroom manager in the Belden Village Mall area hired me. It was another catalog showroom store, and I became the display coordinator.

For the following five and a half years, my life consisted of working full time and taking care of my mother. My mother treated me more like a servant than a son. I had no personal life or friends to do things with. I focused on work and my mother's needs and did not think about finding my father.

In December of 1996, the store I worked for went out of business. During the final days, I overheard a couple of coworkers talking about a Giant Eagle grocery store hiring for their new store. I went and applied, and a manager hired me on January 16, 1996. I started part-time, but after a few months the store manager made me full-time.

Early one morning that winter, I was heading home after working all night. Heavy snow had fallen, and I stopped at a convenience store to get a few groceries for my mother.

When I started to turn left, a snow pile blocked my view. I was hit by another car on my driver's side. I was not seriously hurt, but it made me think about my life. Here I was, 42 years old and still living with my mother. I decided to do something for myself that day. I began to look for a place where I could meet single women.

One Sunday morning, I read an article in the *Canton Repository*. Two churches had a singles ministry, and so I decided to visit one of the churches. I got lost looking for the first one, and so I went back home. I decided to try the other church, which was in the city of Canton. I started to go to a singles volleyball game each week.

The meetings were held at the Church of the Savior, the church that former President William McKinley had attended. I learned that the church was built in 1817. It was a large church and had a gymnasium built into the upper section. It was there where I started to play co-ed volleyball on Tuesday evenings. There at the games, I was able to be myself and act silly when we played.

After a few weeks, one of the girls introduced me to her best friend, Rita. We began dating, and after a few months we fell in love. At first, my mother did not mind my dating a girl, but things changed at home as I fell in love with her.

In 1997 about a year had passed, and I began thinking about marriage. My beloved had a daughter, Ashley, from an earlier marriage. I learned that her birth father had passed away from brain cancer. I began to include Ashley when I spent time with her mother. We would go to places like fairs so she could have fun.

While I was in love with Rita, I also cared about her daughter as a father would.

One evening during a volleyball game, I planned to propose to Rita. I had a friend have a camera ready, and during a break between games, I made my move. I got down on one knee and proposed with flowers and a ring. She said yes, and everyone was excited. I was also thrilled.

However, my mother was quite upset, and my living at home became difficult. My mother had conditioned me throughout my life to stay with her when she knew I should have been on my own. She insisted that I break up with Rita and stay with her. My mother quoted the scripture about children obeying their parents. I told her that I was not a child anymore.

One night when I was trying to decide whether to get married or please my mother, I had a dream. I was standing in a green field with only grass around me. Then I looked up into the blue sky that had no clouds. I saw a young woman flying slowly past me in the air. She had a long white robe on, and she had long blond hair. She turned to her left to look at me. I could tell that it was my grandmother who had passed away in 1984. My grandmother said to me that it was okay to get married.

After my dream, I became determined to get married, but I knew that I needed to live on my own first. Once I found an apartment, I told my mother that I was moving out. She was not happy, but she gave up trying to convince me to stay with her.

Although I was now living alone, I was busy working and planning my marriage and dating. Once I moved out on my own, I became estranged from my mother. I never had time to experience a single life because I was busy working or planning my marriage.

I was hurt because I realized how much my mother had kept me dependent on her. Rita and I had to go through a meeting with the pastor before being married. The pastor recommended that I invite my mother to our wedding, but I refused to ask her. I was aware that I should forgive my mother, but I could not overcome my emotions.

I was married at the Church of the Savior in Canton on February 12, 1998. I chose Valentine's Day, so I would never forget the anniversary. I dressed in a white tuxedo, and my bride wore a white gown.

Although my mother's relatives came, no one would talk about my father when I asked them.

After our wedding, we went on our honeymoon. My wife's parents watched Ashley while we were gone. The evening of our first day of marriage was when I first experienced sex because I was still a virgin. While I did not have a mother or father teach me about sex, everything seemed to come naturally.

Ashley became my stepdaughter, and she was five years old when I became her father. I wanted to adopt my stepdaughter after our marriage, but the current law said I had to wait two years.

I discovered that I could be a father, even though I did not have a father as a role model. Being a father was not so difficult because I had been a part of Ashley's life for a couple years when I was dating her mother.

Soon after our marriage, I told my wife that I wanted Ashley to have a better education than I had. I explained that I could afford to either look for a bigger home for us to live in or send Ashley to a Christian school. We decided to send Ashley to Heritage Christian school. The school was several miles from our home, but I saw to it that Ashley was driven to school each morning for the next decade. I wanted my daughter to have a better education than I received when I grew up in a public school.

My first search – 1999

After my first wedding anniversary, I began to think about my own father, now that I was a father myself. I joined a family history site, Ancestry, to see if I could find information about him.

For the next seven months, I worked on a family tree for my dad. Unlike most people, I only had my parents' names in my tree and my mother's parent's names. After some time, I received some clues that came from other members.

My mother and her family knew my father and his family for around six years. Unfortunately, nobody ever told me anything about my father except that he served in WWII.

Throughout the spring and summer of 1999, I learned more about my dad than I ever had. I discovered that he was born in Lima, Ohio. I found old census records, and I realized that my father had a sister named Helen. I also found out my father's parents were William and

Lena Beach.

I emailed several other Ancestry members who had Beach for their last name. Unfortunately, they had no information about my father. I was able to find a copy of my father's birth certificate. Although I learned some information about my father's relatives, I found few details about my father.

I did not concentrate a lot of time on my search, because I kept busy working and taking care of my wife and daughter. They were my primary focus then.

In September of that year, I wrote a letter to the National Archives and Records Administration. I sent them a form needed to search for my father's military service record. I was disappointed to be told that they could find no records of my dad's service in World War II.

After seven months of searching, I decided to give up trying to locate my father. I did not realize then that while I tried to find my father, he was slowly dying of throat cancer. It would be another decade before I would begin my quest again to locate my father.

Fatherhood

Several weeks before the turn of the century, I took steps to adopt my stepdaughter, Ashley. I had several of my friends write a letter to the court about my character. Because I was excited to adopt my daughter, I appealed to the court several weeks before my second wedding anniversary.

I appeared before the judge in the family court with my wife, Rita. He looked over my request and character witness testimonies. I told the judge that I loved my stepdaughter as if she were my own. He smiled and allowed me to give Ashley my last name. It was one of the best days of my life.

During the winter of 2000, my wife and I decided to try and have a baby. It took several months before we got a positive result from a test. When Sarah was born, I realized that God had arranged for my wife to become pregnant when she did so that Sarah would be created.

My passion for investigating or discovering led me to research how a baby develops in the womb. Some experts believed that speaking or playing music helps a baby's mind grow better. I went to a local toy store and bought a compact disc player with classical music on it. The player had a unique device that I could attach by suction to my wife's stomach. For the last few months of Rita's pregnancy, we would play classical music and talk to Sarah with a microphone while her body was developing.

On the morning of January 8, 2002, Rita gave birth to our daughter, Sarah. I was in the delivery room to videotape the birth. I could hold Sarah shortly after her birth. It was an emotional experience to have our newborn baby in my hands.

A few months later, I got an outside phone call at work. It was my mother, to my surprise. She said she heard that I had a baby. We talked for a while, and I told her that I would bring my family and meet her.

For the first time in my life, my mother acted like

she was proud of me. For the past four years, I had not contacted her. I was hurt about how she had made me dependent on her throughout my life. As we spoke, I realized that I had to forgive my mother.

Shortly after we reconciled, my mother called me one day and told me that she wanted to buy a whole-house air conditioning system. She said she wanted me to have a comfortable house for my daughters. I was surprised but accepted her offer. She paid for everything out of the savings she had.

For the next three years, my mother and I had a normal mother and son relationship. I learned that Mom had moved into an apartment, made friends, and had a good life.

Although my mother never said she was proud of me, I could tell by her actions. Even so, my mother never revealed what happened between her and my father. I knew from experience growing up that asking about my dad over and over was pointless, although I tried.

Problems

In the spring of 2005, I talked with my wife about looking into buying a larger home. We decided that it would be possible with our two incomes. We started to look for a home on days when we were both off.

My wife was excited, as were Ashley and Sarah. We liked one home so much that we signed a letter of intent to buy. However, after I did some research, I realized there were some issues with the land. Fortunately, the real estate agent allowed us to change our minds without losing any money.

One morning, after a few weeks of looking for a home, my wife said she no longer wanted to buy a new home. I asked her why, but she only said that she was not interested anymore. From that fateful day onward, our marriage's love, passion, and happiness slowly weakened like a flower does when it does not get enough water and sunshine.

One day in the summer, I got a phone call at work. A

nurse from a local hospital informed me that neighbors in the apartment building where my mother lived had heard her crying out for help. Neighbors found my mom lying on her living room floor. She had fallen down the previous day but could not get up. By the time I could see my mother, an ambulance had taken her to the hospital.

When I made it to where she was, I found her sitting in a wheelchair in the hallway. She had learned she probably had dementia. Then she told me about her encounter with an orderly.

While she was sitting in the hallway waiting for test results, a young man came over to her. She told me that he had blond hair and was tall and dressed like an orderly. He knelt beside her wheelchair and talked to her about Jesus Christ. He asked her if she was ready to meet the Lord and led her through a prayer of salvation. My mother asked him what his name was, and he told her that it was Gabriel.

Then he left, and she never saw him again. When I went back home, I began to wonder if the orderly was an angel from heaven. I believed that maybe God sent an angel to make sure my mother was ready to go to heaven because God knew she would soon lose her memory.

Before I left the hospital, a doctor told me that I might have the Alzheimer's gene. She explained that there was a chance that I could get the same disease as I grew older.

By the time Ashley and Sarah had their birthdays in

2006, My wife had become more unhappy. I began to see a Christian counselor in our town to make my wife happy and discover what was wrong with me.

The first five months of 2006 were also stressful for our marriage as my mother's dementia worsened. It was difficult to visit my mother in a nursing home since I knew there was no hope for her, and I had to watch as her memory slowly faded away.

Throughout my life, I wished I had a mother who cared for and treated me like a mother should. For the past three years or so, we had had a normal mother and son relationship. Now I had to watch her slowly die of dementia. By springtime, my mother could no longer recognize us when we came to visit.

On Sunday, May 22, 2006, my wife and I visited my mother in the evening at her nursing home. My mother was near death, and she had difficulty remembering me.

After our visit, we returned home that evening. In the middle of the night, I received a phone call from the nursing home. A nurse told me that my mother had died peacefully in the night. It was difficult going back to sleep.

The next day I went to the nursing home to collect my mother's belongings. When I had learned my mother would subsequently die of Alzheimer's, I began thinking about funeral arrangements. I had a copy of her will and life insurance. Unfortunately, my mother only had a $2,000 life insurance policy from New York Life Insurance. She had taken it out after World War II;

however, she did not have a life insurance policy that grew over time.

Fortunately, my mother was a veteran, and I had proof of her military service. I went to the Reed Funeral home in my hometown.

The funeral director there helped me arrange for my mother's burial in Western Reserve National Cemetery in Rittman, Ohio. I still had to use some of my own money to pay for the services.

Since it would be a week before the Western Reserve national cemetery could bury my mother, I had time to notify her relatives. After my marriage in 1998, I had lost touch with most of my mother's relatives since we lived hundreds of miles apart.

My company allowed me to have several days of paid bereavement leave, so I prepared for my mother's funeral on May 30, 2006. During the calling hour from 11 am-12 pm, friends from work and church came to pay their respects. Several of my cousins were there. Uncle Charles and Aunt Glenna also came.

I walked over to my aunt and thanked her for coming. I told her that my mother never would say to me why she and my dad separated. I explained that my mother only said they separated and were never divorced. I asked Aunt Glenna if she would tell me the truth now that my mom had died. She looked at me with a look of sadness; she could only say that it was a sad situation. I was frustrated that after a half century my mom's sister would still not tell me why my parents had separated.

I knew my parents got married in 1948, and I had an old photo of my dad sitting with my mother's family one Christmas. Even though my relatives knew my dad for over five years, no one would say a word about him.

The time came then for my church pastor, Mike Dennis, to have the funeral service. He talked about my mother and her service to our country in World War II. After the calling hour, I followed the hearse up to Western Reserve National Cemetery in Rittman, Ohio.

After the committal service inside a pavilion, a soldier took the American flag that draped my mother's casket, folded it, and gave it to me as he knelt before me. Then the honor guard gave the traditional twenty-one-gun salute.

My oldest daughter, Ashley, was 13 then, and my youngest daughter, Sarah, was only 4.

After we had returned home, I thought about my father, and I wondered where he was. However, I did not try searching for him on my computer again. I focused on working and being a father and husband.

Caring for my mother as she was dying of Alzheimer's had been stressful. The stress of caring for my mother, combined with working full time and being a husband and dad, seemed to weaken the bond between my wife and me.

I spent the next two and a half years going to a Christian marriage counselor when I had time. I tried to figure out how to be the "perfect husband" and make my wife happy and strengthen our marriage. The romance we once had was slowly fading away. Although I worked full time, I spent the last two years of our marriage keeping up with the laundry, and when I had the time, I would cook meals for our family. I did not want to have my marriage fail as my father did and his father before him.

Marriage problems

~

In 2008 my marriage was continuing to fall apart. My wife grew more unhappy, so I went to a Christian counselor in a small town called Dover, about a half-hour drive from home. I spoke to a woman counselor named Sandy.

Because I worked full time, I usually saw my counselor one evening each week. I realized that my marriage was growing weaker, and the romance was already gone. I thought about my parents and how their marriage failed after I was born. I tried to stop history from repeating itself. Still, I told Sandy that I was unable to follow in my father's footsteps.

By the time I turned fifty-six on Halloween, I could tell that the love my wife once had for me was gone. I continued seeing my marriage counselor, hoping that I could still save our marriage.

My youngest daughter, Sarah, turned 7 on January 8, 2009. The following weekend, I was getting ready for work in the morning. My wife was sitting on our bed with our daughters beside her. She told me that she wanted a divorce and that I was to move out quickly

I could tell she was serious. I tried to discuss having a trial separation so that we could work things out. I had to go to work that fateful day, so I agreed to start looking for a new place to live. My wife told me that I was to sleep on the couch each night until I moved out.

It was challenging to work that day and for several weeks afterward. Several of my female coworkers gave me hugs and supported me, and my front-end manager was very understanding. I often worked as a cashier but tried to spend as much of my shifts as possible outside collecting shopping carts, so I did not have to deal with customers.

I could not act as happy and friendly as a cashier should be. Waves of grief and sorrow washed over my soul throughout each day and for many months afterward.

I called the Guiding Grace counseling center and explained that my wife was divorcing me. Sandy made an emergency opening for me to come to see her that week.

One evening after work, I started driving down to see Sandy after my divorce began. I experienced a sense of deep sadness and sorrow as dark as the night sky around me. I felt like a failure. As I drove down Interstate 77 that evening, I considered crashing my car and ending my life. I thought about my father and that now my marriage was also ending.

I was a few miles away from the counseling center when I saw a bridge up ahead going over the interstate. I thought about driving my van into one of the columns that held up the bridge. I quickly reasoned that I would fail at the attempt and wind up only getting injured. I realized what my death would do to my two daughters.

I reminded myself of what I went through when my dad left me. I decided that night to do whatever I could not to walk away from my daughters as I believed my father did from me.

My Christian counselor, Sandy, listened to me as I shared my feelings. She was already aware of our marital problems from earlier sessions. She recommended that I see a lawyer to protect my rights as a father. Sandy shared a method that could save a marriage when a couple was on the verge of a divorce. It was a technique that helped save her marriage.

What Sandy taught me was too late to save my marriage because both spouses had to be willing to try the mental technique. In my case, my wife had already given her heart to another man. I share the method now in hopes that other families can be spared the sorrows of divorce.

The way to save a marriage or close friendship where both persons can no longer stand each other involves using only your mind. When you wake up one morning, find just one thing that you like about the other person. It could be their smile or that they take out the trash or even something small.

On day one, think about that one thing you like throughout the entire day. On day two, find another something you admire or like about the person you cannot stand. Dwell the whole day on those two things. Each following day you add one more thing or attribute to your list.

Sandy explained that one day, you will wake up and find the love that you thought had died between you and your partner will be as strong as it was at the beginning of your relationship. She told me that she tried it for herself when she was unhappy in her marriage, saving their marriage.

As I was driving home, Sandy called my home and left a message for my wife. She told her that I had talked to her and that she was praying for us. I felt hopeless, knowing that I would soon have to leave my two precious daughters.

Sandy talked with my family doctor about my situation. For the following three weeks, they put me on a suicide watch. Usually, I would have to schedule a counseling session. However, for those three weeks, I could call, and Sandy would make time for me whenever I needed to talk.

Twice a week, I would drive a half-hour south in the evening in my old Ford Windstar van to see my counselor. I would listen to old love songs on cassettes because they helped ease the terrible pain I felt inside. I listened to Sandy's advice about getting an attorney and not giving up on being a part of my daughters' lives after divorce.

Since my company had legal insurance, I met with an attorney. He recommended I file for divorce first to protect myself. I told him that I believed I could reason with my wife and agree to a trial separation. Little did I know that she had already organized the divorce, including the paperwork, weeks before.

Several days later, in January, I drove my wife to meet with her attorney. I felt under pressure at the meeting, but I started to sign the divorce agreement. Then I saw that the lawyer did not include my rights as a non-custodial father in the separation agreement. I stopped and refused to finish signing the various documents when I realized I would not be given vacation weeks in the summer with my daughters.

I left the attorney's office and drove my wife home. We did not talk as she was upset with me. From that evening until I finally moved into my apartment, I had to sleep on our living room couch.

During the following two weeks, while I looked for a new home, I also tried to work full time. I found it difficult to be outgoing, knowing that my marriage ended like my father's marriage.

It took me a couple of weeks to find an apartment and arrange the date to move; my wife and I still went to church and sat in the same Sunday school class, which was awkward. However, since I had gone there for eight years, I decided not to go somewhere else. Our friends and pastor offered to talk with my wife; she would not agree to discuss our divorce.

Each day, while I was still at home, my youngest

daughter Sarah would follow me throughout the house, saying, "I love you, Daddy." A decade later, there are times when I remember her words and the sorrow she must have felt knowing that I had to leave. I explained that I did not want to go, but I had to because Mommy no longer loved me.

At the start of the last week of January in 2009, I finally decided on a new place to live by myself. I decided it would be easier on my two precious daughters if they were at school when I finally had to move out.

After working overnight on Thursday, January 31, 2009, I left work to go to my home for the last time. The weather was cold, and a blanket of snow covered the ground. The night manager, Brian, followed me with his truck. When we came into my wife's home, she seemed happy and acted friendly towards us. I already had most of my belongings packed so that it would not take long.

Brian and I loaded up my belongings, and then we left for my new home, which was only a few miles away. I just had a bed and a dresser given to me by a couple, Tim and Cindy, from my Sunday school class, and an old couch. A couple of days before I left my home, a close friend at work, Bob, and his wife Peggy gave me a lovely dining table for my new home.

I had a used Ford Windstar van, which allowed me to move quickly. Brian helped me bring my few possessions up to my second-floor apartment. I thanked my friend for all his help, and then he went home.

For the first time since my childhood, I was utterly alone. It was then that the reality struck me that my marriage was truly over. Unlike most people who reach age fifty-six, I was experiencing being alone on my own for the first time. By this time, I had accepted that my wife and I were no longer "one flesh," as the Bible said marriage was between couples in Matthew 19:4-5. The pain that I felt inside that day was indescribable.

It felt like I was living out in real life a scene from the *Indiana Jones* movie. It felt like my heart was being ripped out of my body as the high priest did to Indiana Jones. When I went to lie down on my bed to rest, I found myself filled with a level of grief and sorrow I had never felt before.

Tears flowed like rain, and for several hours, and I could not get out of bed. I felt like I had not only failed as a husband and father but that I had failed God. I cried so much my chest hurt. I could accept that my wife hated me, and we would never be together, but knowing my two precious daughters loved me still but could not be with me hurt more than words could express.

It took a few hours, but eventually, I experienced the reality of the Bible verse, Matthew 5:4. I was able to get out of bed and get something to eat for supper. I found out that when we go through tough times, the Lord will comfort us and give us the strength to keep going. I accepted that day; I had to admit that my wife would never return to me.

However, I decided not to give up and walk away

from my children, as I believed my father had done to me. I hired a lawyer and started to take legal action to get a good divorce that included a noncustodial father's fundamental rights.

Legal problems

After I moved into my apartment, I was kept busy working and dealing with my divorce's legal issues. Since I had no legal rights to visitation with my daughters, I spent my evenings alone. I realized that my wife's boyfriend did not want me to have time with my children. I began to remember what my childhood was like after my father left. It made me determined not to walk away from my two precious daughters, as my dad did to me.

When I moved into my apartment, I let my wife have our computer. On March 16, I went to the North Canton Library in North Canton, Ohio. The library had computers that the public could use with their library card. There I set up an account on Yahoo to communicate with my friends from church and my ex-wife.

For the next three months, I searched for information about my father at the library when I had time. I had to spend much of my free time in court appearances and meetings with my divorce attorney. I wanted to spend more time researching my dad, but my focus was on my struggle to see my two daughters and to try and get shared parenting in the divorce my wife wanted. I discovered that I had to use my paychecks to pay for the legal bills. That forced me to use my two credit cards to pay for groceries and gas for my van.

My ex-wife and her lawyer insisted that I accept the separation agreement they had prepared, which denied me summer visitation rights. All I had to do was to agree, and there would be no more legal costs.

At the beginning of May, I learned that our city offered a free mediation service to couples going through a divorce. I was able to convince my ex-wife to try mediation. Unfortunately, after several meetings, the mediator told me that it was either her way or else. Therefore, I had to continue the legal process.

During the first week of May that year, a friend at my church told me about a divorce support group at another church. It was a non-denominational church in a small town about twenty miles from my home. They had a three-month course. Phil was the leader of the support group, and he was also an Ohio state police officer.

We met once a week and listened to videos of Christian divorce counselors. Phil gave me a workbook that helped me to express my feelings. It was a helpful addition to my weekly meetings with my counselor, Sandy. I learned that it was reasonable to feel negative emotions as a Christian.

I told my friends and my counselor that the worst part of the divorce was that I could not legally see my two precious daughters. I felt like my daughters were being held hostage by a man who did not love them. I found it challenging to go for several days to a week without contact with my daughters.

The start of the search

Now that I was experiencing first-hand the pain of being separated from my children, I became even more determined to find my father. I wanted to know the truth about why he left and tell him that I understood how going away hurt him. I felt the need to say to him in person that I forgave him.

At the end of May, I was able to buy a used computer and screen for my apartment. On June 21, 2009, I became a member of Ancestry again and searched for my dad and family. Besides working full time, I also often spent time in court, trying to get a non-custodial father's fundamental rights.

Within two days online, I found the first clues about my father and his family. I discovered family secrets that my mother kept from me for over half a century.

The best part of Ancestry.com was that their program searched for clues about my father every day by finding relevant information from research done by other members worldwide.

I soon realized that my father was born just thirty-six days before the start of World War One. In just a matter of days, I learned more about my father and his family than in my entire life until then.

Divorce problems

Like water to a thirsty man in a desert, I found each clue about my father left me wanting to know more. Unfortunately, I spent most of my free time negotiating a shared parenting form of divorce with my wife. Still, she refused and insisted on the separation agreement that her boyfriend's lawyer had written up.

I disagreed because the documents denied my fundamental rights as a non-custodial father. My wife and the other man assumed that I would just go along with whatever type of divorce agreement they wanted. Still, I refused to give up my visitation rights.

I continued a legal battle that would last eighteen months before a judge would grant a fair divorce agreement. I knew first-hand what happened to a child growing up without a father. I became determined to fight for the right to be a father to my daughters, no matter the cost. The end of my marriage and the ensuing divorce became the catalyst for my search for my father.

After four months of negotiating a shared parenting divorce agreement with my wife, I decided to hire an attorney. In July of 2009, I hired a female attorney in my hometown. My company supplied a form of legal insurance that gave me a discount. I had to use my paycheck to pay my part of the legal fees, which made me go further into debt.

My attorney, Beverly, told me that she did not believe the separation agreement I had partially signed in February was fair or legally binding. However, she explained that legal matters could take weeks or months to resolve. By this time, my total debt had climbed to over $13,000. I decided to try to go to court to seek a fair legal divorce that would include summer visitation with my daughters.

One-fourth of my weekly paycheck was taken for child support for my daughters. My monthly rent took another fourth of my monthly pay. I realized that to continue my struggle for shared parenting, I would go deeper into debt.

I wondered if my father had been in a comparable situation when his marriage fell apart. I knew from the one photo of the two of us that my dad loved me. That proved to me that he did not leave me because he stopped loving me.

I now experienced the terrible pain of divorce. I was separated from my two precious daughters, reunited briefly, and then torn apart again. I could understand then how he might have felt it would have been less painful on me if he left and never returned.

On Wednesday morning, August 16, 2009, I went to the Stark County Family Court for a court appearance with a judge about our divorce. I met my attorney, Beverly, at the Stark County Court House. We went through the security checkpoint.

I had never been in an actual trial before as a plaintiff. My attorney and I sat only a few feet away from my wife and her attorney.

I had seen many trials on television shows over the years. However, the stress of giving testimony and being cross-examined was unlike anything I had experienced before. My wife presented her version of how I partially signed the separation agreement in February. My attorney effectively cross-examined her.

However, my wife did not waver from her story. When the opposing attorney cross-examined me, I became tense and nervous. I felt like I was living out a scene from *Perry Mason*. The attorney was intimidating, and my speech faltered sometimes. I tried to explain how I felt coerced into signing the first agreement.

My attorney explained to the judge that the separation agreement should be void because I did not sign all the papers. During the hearing, Beverly tried to submit an email from my ex-wife as evidence. The email showed my wife threatened not to allow me to see my daughters until I signed the papers her attorney drew up. The judge accepted the evidence but did not read it.

I got the impression the judge was not sympathetic

to my case. When the trial was over, the judge told us he would give his ruling later. I left the courthouse emotionally drained. After the hearing, I went to the First Church of the Nazarene in town to speak with my pastor. Pastor Dennis made an appointment for 7 pm for us to talk.

After our meeting, he allowed me to spend some time in the sanctuary. The sanctuary was empty and dimly lit. I went to the altar and spent about a half-hour praying and crying. I told God that I tried so hard to save my marriage, and I did not want to follow in my father's footsteps with a failed marriage. I felt like a failure both to God and to my family.

The following day, the judge in our case made his decision. He decided that I did not prove my case of being coerced into signing the separation agreement. Even though I had not signed all the necessary documents, the judge ruled the separation agreement was valid. The following day Beverly informed me that I had until September 1 to appeal the decision or let it stand. Knowing how it felt to have a father who did not fight to stay a part of their child's life, I decided to appeal.

My attorney, Beverly, filed an appeal three days later, on Saturday, August 19, 2009. The presiding judge set a hearing date for my request on October 19, 2009, at 9:40 am.

I knew doing so would put me deeper into debt if I did this. However, I refused to give up on my daughters. I made up my mind to never let another man who had no love for my two precious daughters spend every day with them, while I had to go up to a week at a time with no visitation.

In the weeks leading up to my appeal, I spent my evenings before bed searching for my dad on Ancestry. On Thursday evenings, I would drive to Dover, Ohio, to spend an hour with my Christian counselor, Sandy.

Further research

~

When I had a set goal, I realized that I could focus and continue working no matter what obstacle came my way. I searched for clues about my father in the evenings. I slowly continued to find clues about my father and his family. Since I had a computer with a small processor and only dial-up internet, finding clues took time.

I discovered that my grandfather, William Edward Beach, was a wealthy accountant for the Sohio oil company in Lima, Ohio. I found that when he was seventeen, Buffalo Bill's Wild West Show came to his hometown in Meadville, Pennsylvania. I did not know that Buffalo Bill had ever traveled to Pennsylvania. My grandfather was able to see famous performers from the wild west, such as Sitting Bull, Annie Oakley, and Calamity Jane.

After I learned that my father grew up in Lima, Ohio, I decided to take a day off and travel there before my appeal in October. Lima was 157 miles away from where I lived. I knew that I could not afford to stay overnight at a hotel, so I planned a one-day trip. My father's birthplace was only about seventy-eight miles from Dayton, Ohio, where I was born.

I learned from my research that Lima was one of the world's largest producers of school buses. I was surprised to discover that when my dad served in England during World War II, Alan Jardine was born in Lima on September 3, 1942. When Al Jardine became nineteen years old, he moved to California, where he became one of the Beachboys. Since my grandfather was a prominent Lima society member, I wondered if my father knew the Jardine family after returning from the war.

On a warm, sunny day in late September, I drove my old Ford Windstar van to Lima, Ohio. I left early to have a few hours to search for clues before returning home. Upon arriving in Lima, I went to the local public library. I told a librarian that I was searching for my father and relatives, and she showed me their Genealogy department.

There, I used a microfilm machine to search through old copies of the local newspaper. I was surprised to learn that my father's parents were quite well off financially during the 1920s and throughout the Great Depression.

I learned that my grandfather fell in love with Lena Fleer. They were married on February 19, 1916, in Minnesota, and then they moved to Lima, Ohio, to live in an apartment building.

At the library, I saw one newspaper article that gave details about my grandparents' divorce. It said that a judge had scheduled my grandparents the following day for a contested divorce case in common pleas court in February of 1929. I wondered if divorce ran in my family, since it also happened to my father and myself.

Before leaving Lima, I visited the grave of my grandfather at the local cemetery. I also saw the grave of Lauren Beach. During my research, I discovered that my grandfather had been married before meeting my father's mother. According to a newspaper article from the library, in 1895, my grandfather had married Ida Belle Crane. They had a son a year later whom they called Lauren.

After leaving the cemetery, I had time to drive by the home where my father had grown up. Unfortunately, the original house he grew up in was gone. The city had replaced it with a row of townhouses.

I returned home with more knowledge about my father's past.

The following month, before the Stark County common pleas court hearing, I searched for more clues about my father. I found records of my dad's military service in World War II. Unfortunately, such records were not legal proof of service.

Pieces of the puzzle of my past started to come together. I was learning more about my father in just a few months than I had the past fifty-seven years.

Visitation

Although only a separation agreement was legal, my ex-wife allowed me to have time with my youngest daughter, Sarah. Every Wednesday afternoon from 5 pm to 8 pm and every other weekend, I spent my time with Sarah. I helped her to learn to read and with her schoolwork.

My apartment was close to a railroad that ran between my apartment complex and Interstate 77. Sometimes we would watch the train go by, and the conductor would throw out candy for her. When the tracks were empty, we would go for a walk. Sarah enjoyed nature, so I became a member of the Akron and Cleveland Zoos.

By this point in my divorce, my oldest daughter Ashley was busy with school and working, so I did not have time with her.

I had to use my credit card because of the legal bills, but I was determined to give Sarah the childhood memories I never had.

During the first week of October, I received a reply from another member of Ancestry.com. He said his name was Scott and that he had a clue about where my father might be living.

I thanked Scott for his help. However, I was both happy and sad. For the first time in my life, I had a vital clue of where my father was. Unfortunately, I also learned shortly afterwards that my father was dead. My dream throughout my entire life had been to find my father alive and to learn the truth about my parents' separation.

On Monday morning, October 19, 2009, I woke up and got dressed for my final appeal. I grew up assuming my dad never fought to be part of my life. Knowing that drove me back to court again. I met my attorney, Beverly, at the Stark County Court House. Once again, we went upstairs to a small courtroom.

My attorney did an excellent job of trying to show that the separation agreement was flawed. This time when the attorneys asked her questions, she only shared dates and her version of events. Unfortunately, the judge refused to look at any of our evidence or even the separation agreement. He ordered that the court make the separation agreement into a legal divorce. However, I was being denied the standard two-week summer vacation time with my daughters.

Of the 88 counties in Ohio, my county was the only one that left the number of summer vacation weeks blank for divorced parents. The judge made his decision at the end of the hearing. He made the divorce final and dismissed us.

As we left the hearing, I thanked Beverly for doing her best. She told me that I could appeal my case to the Ohio Supreme Court. I explained that although I wished that I could do that, I was just too far in debt then. I drove home to my apartment, defeated. I talked to God and told him that I tried hard to save my marriage, not repeat history, but failed.

I refused to leave my daughters as my dad had done to me. The divorce agreement gave me the standard Wednesday evening and every other weekend time with my two daughters. However, I still felt like I had failed them.

A few days before Thanksgiving, I received my copy of the official divorce papers in the mail. I knew that it was unfair and still had time to appeal to the Ohio Supreme Court. However, by then, the legal costs of eight months of fighting for the right to stay a part of my daughter's life had left me with little extra cash. Like in a real war that my dad fought, I had to accept defeat.

I was fortunate to have several good friends at work and church who helped me to keep going. Stan and Esther Summerson, and Gary Nichols encouraged me through emails and shared my concerns and feelings.

The search continues

~

After the judge finalized our divorce, I turned my focus on searching for clues to my father. Finding information about my father and his family was like putting pieces of a giant puzzle together.

One of the men I looked up to growing up was Joe Friday. He was a fictional character in the series *Dragnet*. I developed a love for solving mysteries or searching for clues. My mother would only tell me that my dad served in the army and met him after the war. I started to find more evidence through searching on Ancestry.com. One day I found another record of my father's military service.

I learned more about his military career on that day than in my entire lifetime. On April 8, 1942, my dad enlisted in the U.S. Army Air Corps. He was seventy-one inches tall and weighed only one hundred and forty-eight pounds.

My father went to Columbus to join the Army

Air Force at the Lockbourne Air Force Base. The government activated the base two months later as the Northeastern Training Center for the Army Air Corps. One of the primary uses for the station was to train pilots to fight the Nazis.

I could not find direct proof of what part of the Army Air Corp my father was part of. However, I imagined him as a fighter pilot or a bomber pilot. I also learned that he was an office clerk before enlisting.

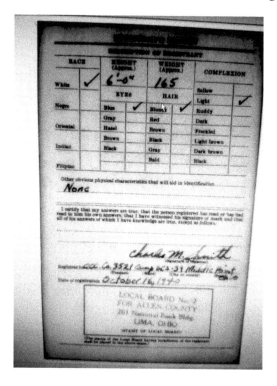

Since I had more free time to search for my father, I set up a family tree online and included my mother and her relatives.

On the evening of Sunday, September 6, 2009, I received an Ancestry member email. Scott wrote to tell me that he had information about my father. He said he had a little luck searching for my father but that it might not be the kind of luck I needed. Scott said he found William Arnold Beach, a social security number and birth date in Ohio. That information matched mine.

Unfortunately, Scott said that my father died on August 6, 1999, in Dallas, Texas. I also confirmed that my father had a sister named Helen, just like my mother's first name.

On October 31, 2009, I turned fifty-seven years old. It was my first birthday without any family in fourteen years.

For the next four months, I continued to search online for clues to my father. I spent every other weekend with my two daughters. I spent my evenings until late searching for information about my father.

While the records about his military service were helpful, I learned that the documents I found would not serve as legal proof of his service.

I began to learn about my father's ancestors from several generations' past.

I discovered that my great grandfather was Lauren Cooper Beach. When he became an adult, he married Mary Bigony in 1864 during the Civil War. Over the next sixteen years, they had nine children. Their first child was a girl who died the day she was born in 1865. They tried again, and the following year, my grandfather was born.

As I traced my father's family tree, I became aware of how important our decisions are and how we can alter the future. If my great grandparents had given up trying to have children when their firstborn had died, I would not exist.

While I learned that my father had spent time in Dallas, Texas, in the 1990s, I still did not know exactly where he might have lived. During the next six months, I continued trying to pinpoint exactly where my father lived in Dallas, Texas.

Divorce Overturned

~

A week before spring began in 2010, I began to think about my two daughters, Ashley and Sarah, and that I did not have any summer vacation time with them.

While sharing my feelings with a friend at work one day, Sandy suggested contacting the Stark County Family Court. In March, while on a break, I called the court office. The secretary connected me to the head of the mediation department.

When the woman in charge answered the phone, I explained my situation to her. I was surprised to hear her tell me that it did not seem right that my divorce did not include any weeks of summer visitation with my daughters. I expected her to politely say that she would investigate my case and hang up. Instead, she checked on her computer about my divorce.

After several minutes the chief mediator told me that the judge should have never approved my divorce. She said the court denied me the fundamental rights of a non-custodial father. Then she said to me that she would look further into the matter and get back to me. I left work that day filled with new hope about my divorce and seeing my daughters.

Upon further investigation, she uncovered that the judge who approved my ex-wife's divorce went to the same church as her boyfriend. Because there was a possibility that the judge and the boyfriend knew each other, the first judge had to step down from hearing any further meetings between my ex-wife and myself. A new judge declared the first divorce invalid.

The following month my ex-wife agreed to attend free mediation meetings with me. There were several meetings between my ex-wife and myself with the mediator over the next few weeks.

Unfortunately, none of my requests for shared parenting or summer visitation was agreed upon by my ex-wife. Since mediation failed, the family court appointed a guardian to evaluate both my ex-wife and me.

The Day Hollywood Came to Akron, Ohio

~

Before a court-appointed guardian began her investigation on myself and my ex-wife, on June 28, I read about a movie being produced in Akron, Ohio.

The film was going to be made by Corbin Bernsen, whom I knew from shows like *L.A. Law* and *Psych*. The news gave information about applying to be a movie extra and said that filming would start in July. Corbin Bernsen had read about how the National Soap Box Derby in Akron, Ohio, was having trouble with funding. He decided to make a movie about the derby to help raise awareness.

On Wednesday evening, July 07, I emailed the movie director. I told her that I would like to be a movie extra and be available on July 25 and 26. I included photos of myself and my daughters.

On Sunday, July 18, the movie director for Corbin

Bernsen emailed me. She informed me that I could be a movie extra and that I would need to be on set early, at 7 am on July 25. I quickly replied to her that I would be there.

The assistant producer told me to bring a snack and drinks and that the filming would be for the entire day. She also said that if I turned in a ticket at the end of the day, she would include my name in the movie credits.

The movie *25 Hill* was written, produced, and directed by Corbin Bernsen. The film was about a young boy, Trey Caldwell, preparing for the All-American Soap Box Derby, held each year in Akron, Ohio.

On Sunday, July 25, I woke up early to get ready for the movie. The area where the filming took place was supposed to stand for Seattle, Washington. Since the movie setting was for spring, the director told me to dress in pants with a light coat even though Akron's weather was warm and sunny.

On Monday, July 26, I got up early in the morning and drove to Akron, Ohio. I arrived early enough to get a parking spot. There were several hundred movie extras along with me. We all met in an area near the road that went past the sports complex.

Corbin Bernsen and the other movie stars were about a block away from most of us. They were near some of the movie props the director used that day.

Corbin thanked us for coming and said that there would be drawings for prizes if we stayed the entire day. The movie director would include our names in the movie credits.

He then explained how they would be shooting and what he needed us to do. Besides being tall, I was also wearing a yellow hat. When Corbin gave directions, he noticed me and referred to me as "the guy with the yellow hat." While I had not planned to stand out in the crowd, it was a wonderful experience to be recognized by a movie star.

The assistant director told us that there would be periods where we would just be on call. One of the main shoots was Nathan Gamble, the star, racing in his soapbox down the roadway. I stood alongside the road with everyone else as Nathan Gamble drove his soapbox down the hill. The camera crew went a short distance in front of him to film him as if he were in a race in Seattle, Washington. I had seen behind-the-scenes reports of movies, but it was fascinating to actually see a film being made.

Later in the afternoon, the director chose me and some other extras to be part of a scene they would record. We were in a park-like setting with picnic tables underneath some trees.

A director told me to sit with two young girls and their grandmother at a picnic table. A short distance away were the movie stars Corbin Bernsen, Nathan Gamble, and Maureen Flannigan, who played the mother. I was excited to be an extra. I felt like I was on a set in Hollywood.

It was also a bittersweet moment for me. The girls who sat at my table reminded me of my daughters,

Ashley and Sarah. Because I had no summer visitation with them, I was not allowed to bring them with me.

The camera crew had finished with their recording. Then everyone took another break as the director prepared to record again.

Then the most amazing thing happened to me. Corbin walked over to the picnic table just several feet away from me. He sat down and started to talk to those of us at our table. I was sitting only a few feet away from a Hollywood movie star! He thanked us for coming and treated us like we were old friends. It was a moment I never thought I would experience.

Corbin Bernsen gathered us all together as a group. He thanked us for helping him make his movie. Then he allowed each of us to stand beside him to get a photo taken.

Since I had nobody with me, another movie extra took a picture of us together. Unfortunately, over time the photo was lost. The movie director told us that they would send us invitations to their world premiere showing *25 Hill* in Akron when the movie was ready.

Twister

On Thursday, September 16, 2010, I drove to see my divorce counselor in New Philadelphia, Ohio. The further south I went, the more it rained. I took an exit that led to a Speedway gas station near Dover, Ohio.

When I pulled up to the station, the rain stopped. I had started to pump my gas when I heard a man yell for everyone to get into the gas station. I looked to my left and was amazed at what I saw. What looked like a tornado was coming straight for me. It had crossed over a four-lane interstate and was heading towards the station.

Then the lights went out in the station. While everyone else had gone inside, I stood mesmerized beside my car. I could feel the wind blowing around me as I stared at what was only a couple of blocks from me.

It seemed like time stood still, and the tornado appeared to stay in one place. I could see the wind swirling inside in a twisting motion. I then saw pieces of shingles and wood flying around inside.

Then I realized that I needed to hide, so I ran inside the gas station. I could feel the wind blowing around me as I entered the station. As I looked outside, I saw a car pull up under the canopy and stop beside a gas pump. I saw a woman was trying to open her passenger side door, but the force of the wind was too strong.

Then I heard her scream for someone to help her and her daughter. On impulse, I opened the door and went towards her car. I could see the whirlwind to my left getting close to the station. Tiny pieces of debris flew around me, and some hit my back as soon as I went outside.

The air pressure must have changed because the car door started to open as I headed towards the car. Seconds later, the wind forced a large garbage can to slide several feet in front of me, and it slammed against the woman's car door.

I reached the passenger side door and opened it up after I moved the garbage can. The mother and daughter quickly ran inside the station. Once we were all inside, the tornado went past the gas station and continued into the nearby town. I was amazed that the station had only minor damage.

When the sky cleared up, I looked outside. Behind the station, I saw a large tree that looked like a peeled banana. The tornado had split the trunk of the tree in several different directions.

I called Sandy, my counselor, to see if it was okay to

see her for our counseling session. She said it was safe, so I went to see her. I told Sandy about my experience and that angels were watching over me.

When I got home that evening, I watched the local news. The fire captain explained that the tornado had torn off the roof of a gas station in town. He said that it was a miracle and a half that nobody was injured.

The Biggest Loser

Shortly after the TV series, *The Biggest Loser* aired on January 4, 2011, my store had its version. Giant Eagle started a program to encourage employees to lose weight and become healthier.

Management designed it like a popular television show. Each week employees who took part had to weigh themselves in front of our front-end manager, Nancy, who kept a weekly record.

There were small rewards each week for those who made progress. Management told us that at the end of a couple of months, the winner would receive a $100 bonus, and second place would be $50.

I joined the local YMCA in North Canton, Ohio. I explained my financial situation, and I was given a scholarship for myself and my youngest daughter, Sarah. I was able to afford the reduced cost, so I started to exercise after work. I also started to buy Subway sandwiches each day. I would eat half of one for lunch and the other half for supper. I discovered that I could focus on reaching the destination when I had a goal with a set deadline.

Over the previous two years, since my divorce began, I had gained over forty pounds and started the contest at just over 250 pounds. Each participant had to lose weight in whatever way they chose.

In my meetings with a Christian counselor a couple of years earlier, I learned that I had a form of ADHD. I also discovered that I could hyper-focus. I became focused on winning the contest. I watched what I ate and exercised every week.

I lost weight during the contest, and in the final two weeks, it came down to a friend of mine, Steve, and myself. In between weigh-ins at work, I would weigh myself at the YMCA.

At the final weigh-in at work, Nancy weighed us and calculated the scores. Although Steve had lost more weight, I came first because the contest was based on the total percentage of body fat lost. I won $100, and Steve won $50.

A New First Cousin

During the last week of January 2011, one of the clues I found on Ancestry revealed that I had a first cousin. Her name was Megan, and my membership allowed me to email her.

On January 30, 2011, I received a reply. Megan told me that she was overwhelmed to learn she has a first cousin she never knew existed. My father's sister, Helen Beach, had grown up to marry Rex Turner in 1940, and they had several children.

Megan told me that her family lived in Oklahoma during the 1950s. I learned that around 1959, my father visited his sister, who was Megan's mother. After my father left, his sister was upset with him because he was not married to the woman he had brought. Megan told me that her mother was like my mother in that she never talked about her side of the Beach family.

Megan and I communicated for a few months. Unfortunately, Megan stopped using Ancestry.com, so I never had a chance to learn more about my first cousin and her family or meet them.

Before I lost contact with Megan, she told me about our grandmother, Lena Beach. My grandmother took my father and sister, Helen, to New Jersey to live after her divorce. I learned that in 1921 my grandmother, Lena Beach, had filed for divorce. According to the news article, she had charged clothing worth $9.70 to her husband's credit. When he found out, she accused him of physically beating her. They had only been married for two years.

Another newspaper article later that year said that my grandparents had reconciled. However, I discovered another article from 1929. It reported that my grandmother had won a divorce from my grandfather.

My grandmother was awarded custody of my father and his sister. My grandfather was awarded visitation, and he had to pay child support of $40.00 a month. Today that amount would be around $630.00.

I also found a copy of the city directory for Lima, Ohio, in 1936. It listed my father, with his name as Arnold William Beach. This information matched my father's name he used when in high school.

Over the past decade, I have learned that my father's ancestors were wealthy, dating back to before the American Revolution. Unfortunately, my grandfather gave his wealth to his son from his first marriage. My father and his sister Helen did not inherit any wealth when their grandfather passed away.

I continued to do research about my grandmother. Before the end of the year, I discovered how my grandmother had died. I found a newspaper article about my father's mother on Ancestry. It was a Copy of *The Daily Home News* from New Brunswick, New Jersey. On the front page was an article about my grandmother, Lena Beach. The newspaper was dated March 24, 1932.

I discovered that my grandmother began walking along a road near Metuchen, New Jersey. According to the newspaper article, a motorcycle driver cut off a man driving his car. When the driver swerved to the right to avoid hitting the motorcycle, he ran into a bank along the side of the highway, overturned, and struck my father's mother. The news article said that she died instantly. My father and his sister were only teenagers when their mother was killed.

After her death, the family of Mrs. Lena Beach buried her in Lima, Ohio. My father and his sister had to stay with relatives for three weeks.

My cousin informed me that when my grandfather was notified that his ex-wife was killed, he did not go and pick up his children in New Jersey. He decided to still go on a three-week vacation trip with a male friend. I was amazed that any father would take a vacation instead of being with his children after their mother had been killed.

In one of our last conversations, Megan told me about her uncle Lauren. He was the half-brother of my father. I discovered that my grandfather, William

Edward Beach, was a thirty-second-degree mason and a "Knights Templar" member.

Megan had told me that Uncle Lauren would visit from his home in Chicago when she was a child. He would give her and her brother expensive gifts and seemed to have a lot of money.

While I never found the last will of my grandfather, I believe that when he died in 1945, he gave most of his wealth to his firstborn son, Lauren. My mother never mentioned that my dad had any money. Therefore, I concluded that my grandfather had not left much to my father after his death.

Divorce Decision

Wednesday, February 09, 2011, was one of the most important days of my life. I got dressed in the morning to go to the Stark County Court House. After passing through security, I met my attorney. We entered the courtroom, where a judge would decide on my new divorce. The court-appointed guardian was also in attendance.

The judge approved my divorce and granted me two weeks of summer vacation with my two daughters. He also allowed me an extra hour with my daughter Sarah each Wednesday, so I had time to take her to church and return her home.

Ironically, the judge approved my divorce two years after my wife first said she wanted a divorce. For two years, I had no summer vacation time with my daughters. However, I was glad that my legal struggles were over, and I could have more time to search for clues about my dad. My belief that my father deserted me made me determined to stay a part of my daughter's life after divorce.

Success

Now that my divorce was finalized, I could spend more time searching for my father. The one small photo of him smiling at me proved he was happy to be my father. I believed that he never returned because he could not handle the terrible pain that a divorced dad suffers on leaving his children every time.

I remembered what my marriage counselor told me that after my divorce started. She explained that I was experiencing the same emotions as military parents do. When parents in the military must leave their children, levels of certain chemicals like serotonin and dopamine in their brain drop for a few days.

Sandy explained that the "feel good" chemicals in their minds are restored when they return to their children. She told me that the same thing happened to non-custodial fathers like me. However, in my case, the time between the rise and fall of these chemicals was too short.

This information helped me understand why my life seemed so empty when I was apart from my daughters and why I was happy when I saw them. Because of my own experience, I empathized with my father and why he left and never returned. I had never felt bitter towards my dad for leaving. I could now understand the pain he experienced being apart from me.

During the second week of March 2011, I made an important discovery about my father. The Ancestry website found a copy of the Texas Death Index, a form that listed everyone who had died in Dallas, Texas, in 1999. In the list was my father's name. His date of death was August 6, 1999.

Several days later, I found a newspaper article online on Ancestry. It said that my father had passed away at Baylor University Medical Center in Dallas, Texas. I contacted one of the staff at the hospital where my father had passed away. The nurse who checked their records told me to go through the Medical Examiner's office in Dallas, Texas.

I called the Dallas County Medical Examiner office and talked to a female medical examiner in the afternoon. She told me that my father died at 7:50 pm of respiratory failure due to branchiogenic carcinoma.

The medical examiner then explained that my father had died alone, without even one friend or family member. Since no one knew about me, and my dad had nobody to claim him, the city of Dallas treated him like a "John Doe." Once my father died, the hospital sent his body to the Dallas County Medical Examiner.

There they verified how my father died.

I was sad to learn he died of lung cancer and that he died alone. She also told me that they put my father's body into a body bag after the examination. At that time, Dallas's city took unclaimed remains of people who died to an old cemetery just outside of town.

It was painful to hear the examiner describe how they dropped my father's body into an open grave. The thought that my father being buried by the city of Dallas with no service or casket filled me with both grief and anger. I decided that day to find a way to bring my dad's body home to give him a proper burial. Nobody deserved to have their body just dropped into an empty grave and buried with no service or headstone.

The medical examiner gave me the contact information to get a certified copy of my father's death certificate. On March 24, I emailed the Bureau of Vital Statistics in Dallas, Texas, asking them for a certified copy of my father's death certificate. Shortly before midnight, I received a reply. The medical examiner also gave me instructions on the documents I needed to fax them. The next day I made a copy of my birth certificate and faxed it to them.

I was thrilled to finally be able to get a copy of my dad's death certificate. With that document, I would be able to bury my dad one day. I was also sad that my dad was not alive so I could find out what happened in 1954.

During the first week of April, I found a notice on

the door of my apartment. It was from the U.P.S., and it told me that there was a package for me. I thought it might be my father's death certificate, so I drove down to the town's central office the next day. I picked up the large envelope that came from the city of Dallas, Texas. The sky was clear that day, with just a few white clouds in the sky. When I opened the envelope to look at my dad's certificate, tiny snowflakes started to fall around me.

I finally had more precise details about my father than I ever had before. I was thrilled and went and bought a photo frame to put the certificate inside to protect it. Now that I had my first legal document about my dad, I made it my goal to keep looking for clues about him and to bring his remains home to Ohio. I knew I had to find proof of my father's military service to give him a military burial that he deserved.

My second time
with Corbin Bernsen

At the beginning of July, I received an invitation from Team Cherokee Productions. The movie director was invited to the world premiere of the movie *25 Hill*. I was excited to be able to go, and I could get the day off work. I knew that this would be as close to being in Hollywood as I would ever get.

On Saturday evening, July 9, I arrived early to find a place to park. The movie premiered at the Akron Civic Center in Akron, Ohio. The center could hold 2,593 people, which was how many people came for this event. I was surprised to see that there was a red carpet inside.

I felt like I was inside a world premiere like I had seen on the news in Hollywood. The ushers seated me in a reserved seat on the balcony for the movie extras.

Corbin Bernsen and Tim Omundson were there

with their wives as well as the other leading actors.

Corbin Bernsen came onto the stage, and everyone clapped loudly. He thanked everyone for coming and talked about the movie and how he wanted to support the soapbox derby. Corbin explained that God had him sit in a specific seat on a plane flight one day. In the back of the chair, he saw an article about the Akron Soap Box Derby. That inspired him to write the script for *25 Hill*.

FACES OF AKRON AND TAFT

ANIE ALBANESE-MAY	JEN ALEXSONSHK	ALYSSA ALEXSONSHK
ANNE ALEXSONSHK	RICK ALEXSONSHK	DEBBIE AMUNDSEN
BARB AMBROSE	CHRIS ANDERSON	MARK AMUNDSEN
JEAN ANDREA	JOHN ANDREA	ALEX ANDREA
ASSANDRA ANDRESS	JOHN ANDRESS	CARLA ANDRESS
STEVE ASHBY	COURTNEY ASHWORTH	KAROLYNN ANDRESS
BRANDY BADER	ABBY MAE BAIRD	TYLER AUSTIN
VICKIE BAKER	PETER BANDOWSKY	DENISE BAIRD
MATTOX BARNETTE	SYDNIE BARNETTE	BOBBIE BARDEN
KAYLA BARTON	DEBBIE BATES	TANGELA BARNETTE
PAMELA BAYLOR	REX BEACH	MARY ANN BATES
DONNA BECKER	JOHN BEERS	PRISCILLA BECK
BILL BELL	BILLIE BELL	BARB BELL
COLE BELLINGER	GRANT BENT	TERRIN BELL
STEVE BERGMAN	DIANE S. BERKHEIMER	MICHALINE BENT
CAROL BERTOLINI	CATIEDIA BERTOLINI	MARK BERRINGER
SANDRA BIRCHFIELD	ALEC BISHEIMER	DANIEL BIRCHFIELD
JOHN BISHEIMER	KATHY BISHEIMER	JIM BISHEIMER
AMY BITTNER-LUDWIG	RACHEL BLOMERLEY	NATHAN BISHEIMER
NORMA BOLDT	APRIL BOLYARD	MACK BOGNER
EMILY BOOK	LEISYL BOONE	CASSIDY BOOK
PATRICIA BOONE	CHRIS BOSAK	LONIE BOONE
DAVID BOSAK	JOEY BOSAK	COLLEEN BOSAK
DAPHNE BOSTON	FLYNN BOSTON	MAX BOSS
TANNOR BOSTON	JASON BOTSFORD	RANDY BOSTON
SAM BOUGHTON	DANNY BOWSET	PAIGE BOUGHTON
JAMES BOWSSON	ELLIE BOXLER	JUSTIN BOWSET

As I watched the movie, I realized that the movie producer did not include the scenes they had filmed of me. I stayed to watch the closing credits and saw my name listed on the big screen, which made me feel good. Before I left, I was able to see the cast of the movie in the main lobby as reporters surrounded them. I went back to my apartment and spent some time looking for clues about my father on Ancestry.com.

The Dark Ages

In the autumn of 2011, the debt from my two-year-long divorces, combined with my car loan and child support obligation, caused me to struggle financially to pay all my bills. Because my divorce proceedings lasted for 24 months, I had to borrow money against my life insurance to pay my legal fees. When I fell behind in paying the loan back in January 2012, I surrendered my $15,000 policy.

Unfortunately, by the time a good divorce was approved by the courts, my oldest daughter Ashley was considered an adult and not required to spend time with me.

Throughout 2012 I could not afford a television cable bill. Therefore, when my youngest daughter, Sarah, nine years old, would spend time with me, I would take her to the public library with free video rentals. There we would pick out movies or television series that she liked.

We would go back to my apartment, where I played them on a VHS player on an old TV set that I had bought from a Goodwill store. I felt ashamed inside that I had to do this, but Sarah was happy, and that was all that mattered. For the following six years, most of my meals were pasta, bologna sandwiches, or hot dogs. Eating at restaurants was a treat I would use when I had time with my daughter.

Each year after my divorce, I would take Sarah to places that she enjoyed and were educational in the summer, such as the zoos in Akron and Cleveland, Ohio, and the Cleveland Science Center. Since we visited these attractions several times each summer, it required a yearly membership to save money.

However, I did not have enough money left after paying my monthly bills to pay cash. Therefore, I had to use a credit card, which made my debt even more significant. I could have saved money by staying around my hometown, but I felt it was essential to give Sarah the chance to learn and experience new things.

It was at the Cleveland Science Center that Sarah learned how to use an escalator. The main floor had a people mover that went down to the lower lobby, which had the food court and other attractions. As we stood at the top on our first visit, Sarah was nervous about taking the first step because the steps were moving quickly. I assured Sarah that it was safe and held her hand as we stepped out onto the first step. After our first trip, she was comfortable using the people mover.

The science center in Cleveland, Ohio, is home to the NASA Glenn Visitor Science Center, which is one of only eleven such centers in the country. One of our favorite attractions there was the Cleveland Clinic Dome Theater. The theater showed films shot in IMAX, which is the world's most oversized film format. We sat under a giant rounded screen that was six stories high and surrounded us not only in front but above and around us. There were oversized speakers with 11,600 watts of ultra-digital sound. The theater also had the world's first giant dome three-projector system that was illuminated by lasers. Watching the movies, I felt like I was inside the film since it surrounded me.

A movie was shown which featured the different objects found through the Hubble Space Telescope using time-lapse photography. I felt like I was on the bridge of the Starship U.S.S. Enterprise. The movie took us on a journey through space. We saw countless galaxies and universes that are billions of light-years away, passing by us not only in the front but also around and above us.

We were able to see new galaxies forming. To myself, I felt like I was watching God create the universe in front of me. The experience was terrific. The pictures were taken of thousands of galaxies, nebulae, and supernovae over 100 million light-years away. We were told that we were seeing galaxies the way they looked 100 million years ago.

The years 2012 through 2013 were hard financially. However, in 2013 the superintendent, Charles Riddle, at my daughter's school met me one day and asked me how long I had been doing volunteer work. I told him I had helped since 1998, when I brought my oldest daughter, Ashley, to kindergarten.

He invited me to come to the next board meeting, so I agreed to attend. When Mr. Riddle asked me to go into the session, I was surprised. The superintendent awarded me with a nice plaque honoring my 14 years of doing volunteer work. Then I was told I could leave but to wait outside.

After the board meeting, Mr. Riddle sat down beside me in the hallway. He told me about a part-time opening as a custodian. Since it was early in the morning, I said yes. I felt that this was an answer to prayer for me. I would now have more income to help pay off my debts, which would get me closer to getting a bank loan to pay for my dad's funeral and buy a home. While I had the goal of meeting my dad, I also dreamed of buying my first home.

For the next three years, I worked at Heritage Christian School at 6 am before working full time at Giant Eagle. I was responsible for getting the school ready for opening each morning. I kept the sidewalks cleared of snow or debris and watched the boilers dating back to 1968.

Working 11 hours or more each day was often tiring, but I was glad to see and talk to Sarah sometimes when I worked at the school. My evenings were still spent searching for clues about my father and his family.

On June 3, 2015, I drafted an email to the Grand

Prairie Genealogical Society found in Grand Prairie, Texas. I asked them if they could find any obituary record for my father or the exact location of my father's grave. Unfortunately, the staff member told me that the cemetery where my father was buried was extensive. The Society did not have any information on locations. The society's chairperson did give me the phone number of the Southland Memorial Cemetery, where they had buried my father.

On June 4, 2015, I contacted the Southland Memorial Park cemetery and spoke to the secretary. I explained to her that I was looking for the exact location of my father's gravesite. She told me that she knew someone who was there when they buried my father. She told me that she would contact him and asked me to call back another day.

I tried to call the following day again but could not get any information. The next time I called, I spoke to the director and gave her information about my father. After I gave her his date of death and social security number, I finally learned precisely where the city of Dallas had buried my father. The director explained how they buried my father. Until then, I had assumed the cemetery his body had just dropped into an empty hole inside a body bag.

I learned, for the first time, precisely what the situation was. When the city buried my father in the cemetery, a member of the Dallas County Medical Examiner's office went also. She said that before the cemetery buried my dad, the medical examiner attached a body tag to his toe, as seen in television shows. They did that for every unclaimed body who died in Dallas, Texas.

Before they lowered my dad's body into an empty grave, the director said they had the gravesite lined with concrete. They placed a concrete slab over the top of the grave. While there was no ceremony or gravestone, they did put a piece of concrete on top with my father's name on it.

A small metal stake was also placed in the ground with a case number for if anyone ever claimed him. I felt different emotions, from grief and sadness to happiness. It also made me even more determined to bring my father's body back home so I could give him a proper funeral and burial.

For the next eleven months, I searched for more clues about my father and his relatives online. I wanted my dad to be buried in our National Cemetery in Rittman, Ohio. However, I needed proof of my dad's military service.

I also focused on paying down my debt. I did not have any savings, and I knew it was hard to get a personal loan. One day I met with a home loan officer about home buying. He taught me a valuable lesson. He taught me to pay only the monthly minimum on large debts or bills. Then I should spend whatever money I had left on paying off the smaller debts, one at a time. By using this method, I was slowly able to improve my credit score.

In May 2016, I went to my local veterans' affairs

office in town. I filled out paperwork and included my father's social security number and some details I had learned from Ancestry.com. The office then searched for any records of my dad's military service. After a few days, a staff member notified me that they found no papers, probably because a fire in 1973 had destroyed them. I was discouraged because I knew that I could never bury my father in our national cemetery without legal proof. I focused on paying down my debts because I knew that a personal bank loan was the only way to bring my dad home.

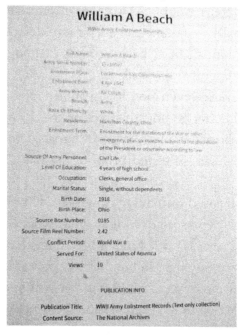

After this setback, I decided to write a letter to President Barack Obama about the new form of music I worked on over the past five years. I shared my new song versions with my friend at school, Dawn. She worked in the security office of the school, where I worked part-time.

For the first two years of my divorce, I would listen to old love songs in my car on the many days I could not see my lovely daughters. Like countless other divorced fathers, I daily felt the pain and loneliness of being separated from my children who loved me.

In the spring of 2011, I watched a movie on TV called *Sister Act*. In the movie, some words of famous love songs were changed. The result was new song versions about a love for God instead of romantic love.

I decided to change some old romantic songs to talk about a parent's love for their children. After five years, I had created two dozen new song versions for divorced families. Dawn told me about a copy center that would edit my letter and print it on professional-looking paper. I uploaded my letter to Lisa Carter's Copy Center in Alliance, Ohio. She was able to print out a professional-looking letter.

In the first part of July 2016, I mailed my letter to President Obama. I included several of the songs I had written. I explained that I believed my new "sad songs" could help comfort non-custodial parents and their children and prevent suicides. I was aware that there were copyright issues over changing the words of famous songs. I thought perhaps President Obama could help make my new form of music a reality.

I knew that any letter to the president goes to a mailroom in the White House for screening. I realized that the chances of my letter reaching the president were slim, but I decided to try anyway.

On Monday, July 25, 2016, I received an email from a Maryland crisis center executive director. He informed me that the White House had received my letter. Unfortunately, whoever screened my message misunderstood my letter when I talked about suicide and referred me to a crisis center near the White House. I replied, explaining that I was writing about how my songs could help prevent suicide. I never received a reply.

The surgery and prayer answered

On July 15, 2016, after work, I went to my local YMCA. When I took my shoes and socks off, I saw an infection in my right foot. I went to a nearby urgent care facility to have my foot checked out. A technician took several x-rays of my foot. Then they had a sample of the infection checked by the lab. After a wait, a doctor came into my room. He told me that the infection had not reached my bone, although it had started to eat away part of the skin on my toe. He wrapped up my toe with a bandage and my right foot with gauze. After a couple of days of rest, I went back to work. I took the medication I was given daily and thought my toe was getting better.

I had already scheduled an overnight stay at the Kalahari Water Park, in Sandusky, Ohio, for my daughters and me. I was happy because this was the first time in over six years that I would spend two whole days with Ashley and Sarah. They were excited about the trip, and I did not want to disappoint them by canceling the trip.

On the last weekend in July, I took both Ashley and Sarah to a nearby water park. I thought my right toe was healing, so I brought a small bottle of a liquid bandage product. We all had lots of fun, especially in the massive wave pool. Unfortunately, I did not realize that a liquid band-aid is not the best protection in a giant wave pool with hundreds of people.

After returning home, I noticed what looked like a scab had formed over where my toe infection had been. On August 4, I went to see a podiatrist. The doctor sat down in front of me and examined my toe using a unique device. He had a look of concern when he then looked at me. He asked me, on a scale of 1 to 10, what level of pain I felt. I told him I felt no pain.

The doctor told me my pain level should have been a 10; however, I felt no physical pain. The doctor explained that the bacterial infection had been slowly eating through the skin on my toe. He explained that the physician who had treated me a month earlier gave me medication for the wrong type of infection. He explained that going to a water park had only made the disease worse.

My doctor told me that the infection had eaten through my toe's skin and that he could see the bone with a special light. He said I needed surgery very soon and that he would have to cut off a piece of the bone to remove the infection, which had attached itself to the bone of my toe and could spread through my body. It was scary to realize that I could lose my leg or even my life.

On Tuesday evening, August 16, I emailed my pastor, Pastor Hanson, about my surgery the next day. He replied that he prayed for me right after reading my email. I had seen God perform miracles over the years, but I was still scared of the surgery. I had not had surgery since I was a young boy when I had my tonsils removed.

Wednesday morning came, and I got up early to go to the hospital. I could not eat breakfast because a nurse would give me an anesthetic that morning. My friend from church, Bill, had arranged to pick me up and take me to the hospital, where the nurses prepared me for my surgery. Bill stayed with me. While waiting to be taken to surgery, Bill prayed aloud for me, which comforted me. After his prayer, I felt relaxed, and my sense of humor returned.

The time came, and an orderly wheeled me into the operating room. The operating room had very bright lights. The anesthesiologist began to give me an anesthetic, so I told him I would close my eyes because the lights were bright.

When I opened my eyes, I looked around and asked a nurse when the doctor would arrive. She told me that the surgery was over, to my surprise.

Bill drove me home after I was out of recovery. My surgeon said the surgery was a success, and the surgeon had removed the infection from my foot. I only lost a small piece of the bone in my right toe.

For the first few days I was home, my close friend, Gary Nichols, delivered home-cooked meals for me from my Sunday School class. Seven days after my surgery, the surgeon removed the dressing from my foot. He told me that I had three diverse types of bacterial infections in my toe. Although my entire toe was several shades of blue, I was just grateful to God; most of my toe was still there. Unfortunately, I learned I could not return to work for several more weeks. My doctor explained that I had to be off work for over five weeks because I could not drive.

My union did supply some financial relief. However, I still had to pay child support every week, even though I could not work. I felt frustrated that every time I thought I could set some money aside to pay to unearth my father and bury him, something happened to put me back.

I decided to email the office of Governor Kasich of Ohio to I ask if he could help me find proof of my dad's military service. On August 31, 2016, I received an email from the public liaison for the Governor of Ohio. She informed me that he could not get involved since it involved the Department of Veterans Affairs. While I was discouraged, the governor's aide gave me the address of two Congress members from the state of Ohio. This information about U.S. Senator Sherrod Brown would play a key role in reuniting my father and me.

I decided to spend some time just resting at home and recovering from my surgery. While I could not drive for six weeks, I kept looking for clues on Ancestry.com. While I did find information about my father, I knew it was not legal proof of his military service. I was still glad to learn more about my dad.

On Tuesday, September 13, 2016, I visited the surgeon who had worked on my toe. Two weeks earlier, a nurse had told me that she thought I would lose my right toe because it did not look well. I had asked my friends at church and on Facebook to pray for me the day before.

My surgeon removed the stitches from my toe. He examined my toe and told me that it was healing correctly. He said to me that I could return to work the following week as a cashier. For the next two weeks, I was not allowed to walk in malls but just at work to enable my toe to heal fully. I was just thankful to God that I still had ten toes and could work and see my daughters.

In October, I was able to work full-time again. However, the loss of six weeks' pay began a type of "ripple effect" financially that would continue for the next sixteen months. I knew that if I fell behind in paying my bills, it could hurt my credit rating. After six years, I realized an unsecured personal loan from a bank was the only way I could ever afford to bring my dad home. My attempts to get help from my government had failed.

Shortly after I returned to work, I told my friend and

co-worker Andrea that I had worn cheap shoes at work for several years. Since I often did chores outside of the school in all sorts of weather and at Giant Eagle, my feet would sometimes get damp from the cold or rain.

I told Andrea that I had little money to spend on myself because I spent my income supporting my daughters and keeping up with my bills, so my credit score would keep rising. I told Andrea that I was focused on helping my daughters and bringing my father home. I had sacrificed my needs for years.

One day. Andrea told me that she would take Sarah and me to a shoe store where she bought her shoes. On a day I had off with Sarah, Andrea drove us to a shoe store. An employee measured my feet, and Andrea paid for a pair of shoes for me. I thanked her and explained that it would be a while before I could repay her. She told me that I did not have to repay her. For the first time in years, I was able to work in top-quality shoes, and they made working easier since I had flat feet and curved toes.

Two days before Thanksgiving 2016, I had to leave my part-time job at Heritage Christian School in Canton, Ohio, for the last time. I lost my job due to the restructuring of positions. My co-workers had a going-away party for me. Several members of the staff gave me comforting hugs. Although I still had my full-time job, the loss of the extra income made it challenging to keep up with all my bills. For over six years, I had been working on restoring my credit rating. My rating had been slowly climbing higher each year.

Less than 24 hours after I lost my part-time job, my store manager gave me what I considered a promotion. My store manager offered me the new position of being a porter. While most people might not think of such a job as a promotion, it felt like it to me. For the past several years, I had spent up to eight hours a day pushing shopping carts up an incline into the store in all types of weather. The combination of working in all kinds of weather and my age often left me exhausted after work. I was so happy to have a position inside the store.

On December 13, 2016, I sent an email to a member of Congress from my state. I explained to him my situation. I told him that the Veterans Affairs Department in my city had tried the year before to do a computer search for my father's military records. They could not find anything and surmised it was because a fire in 1973 had destroyed his files. I learned that on July 12, 1973, the massive fire at the National Public Records Office destroyed over 16 million Military Personnel files. The fire burned most of the U.S. Army records from 1912 to 1960.

Unfortunately, a few days later, I received an email saying that he could not help me.

As the Christmas season approached, I had very little extra money left after my various bills and living costs. I focused on not falling behind on paying bills, so I could continue improving my credit score. Except for when I had time with my daughter Sarah, my meals mainly consisted of pasta, bologna, hot dogs, and french fries.

Even though I no longer worked at my part-time job at Heritage Christian School, I still stopped by occasionally to talk to my friend, Dawn Du Bose. One day I told her about my financial situation. She told me that her husband, Morris, had been promoted to manager at the Total Living Center. It was a Christian soup kitchen that also gave out free food on Sunday evenings.

I thought I would not qualify because I worked full time; however, Dawn helped me realize that I was eligible. Each Sunday evening, around 6 pm, I would drive over to the center. I volunteered to help pass out the free food to the poor and homeless and help clean up afterward. Being a volunteer, I could take home some free groceries. Sometimes I could get frozen meat or chicken that was donated, or bread. Morris Du Bose knew my situation, so he often would give me a meal to take home from the supper they served the people.

For the next two years, after work or spending a Sunday with Sarah, I would go to the Total Living Center to help. I helped clean up after supper and pass out the free food to those in need. Getting some free groceries helped reduce my food costs each month for the next several years. That allowed me to put more of my paycheck into reducing my debt and increasing my credit score.

On December 31, 2016, a car loan manager approved a car loan at Progressive Chevrolet in Massillon, Ohio. After a couple of weeks of looking for a larger car for my daughter and me, a car salesperson, Jim Hall, found me a nice certified used car.

For seven years, I had worked on improving my debt-to-income ratio. I had raised my credit score high enough to qualify for a loan to buy a certified used 2014 Chevrolet Impala. Even though I still owned around $12,000 on the small car, Mr. Hall arranged to trade my old car just before the end of the year.

My credit score was just good enough for one lending company to approve my loan that day. My Impala was the best car I had ever owned. The warranty would save me money on repairs in the future, which would allow me to improve my credit score even more. I was hopeful that the next year would be when I would bring my father's body home.

On January 16, 2017, I mailed a letter I wrote to the President of the United States. I told him about my father and asked him for financial help to exhume my dad and bring him back home. A few days later, I received an email from a staff member at the White House. Only one short paragraph that said my letter was received and sent to the appropriate federal agency. I never heard anything again from any agency, so I became discouraged.

For the next couple of months, I searched for more clues about my father and his ancestors online. However, I gave up trying to get help from the federal government. After six years of trying, it seemed hopeless that I would ever find legal proof of my father's military service, let alone financial help.

Angels on the highway

On the first weekend of March 2017, I spent time with my youngest daughter Sarah. After returning Sarah to her mother to sleep overnight, I started to drive back to my home. I turned left at a stoplight onto Route 62 and began to go over a small hill. I saw the car in front of me turn sharply left into the passing lane. The next second, I saw the figure of a man walking in the middle of my road. He was waving his hands in the air, and when my car lights reached him, I could see that he was young.

I instinctively slammed my right foot on the brake because another car was beside me in the passing lane. My Chevy Impala stopped on a dime just a few feet away from the young man. A split second later, a van behind me slammed into the rear end of my car.

Even though I knew a car had hit mine from behind, I hardly felt the impact. I then gently pulled off the right side of the road around the man in the street to prevent a chain collision from pushing my car into him. I got out of my car to check on the young man. He had collapsed onto the roadway and was lying on his back. Two men had stopped their vehicles from the other side and had put their coats on him.

I called 911 on my cell phone as I stood in the passing lane of the highway. I felt like I was living out a scene from a movie. The woman who had struck me from behind asked me if I was okay, and I told her I was. Then the young man who was still on the road screamed out that someone had stabbed him in the back.

I called 911 back to give the operator more details and inform them that the man had said someone attacked him. I was amazed that several sheriffs' cruisers and an ambulance arrived on the scene in just a couple of minutes. By then, the man was lying on the roadway, thrashing back and forth, and I saw white foam coming from his mouth. I sat in my car to write out a report, but I found it difficult to breathe at first. A sheriff told me that he would not give me a ticket because he would cite the woman who hit me for driving too close. The deputy sheriff said to me that the accident damaged my car's rear bumper. Once I made it home, I came to believe that God had placed me on that road that night, so I would be driving slow enough to save the young man's life.

Making progress

A few days after my accident, I decided to contact U.S. Senator Sherrod Brown by email. Unfortunately, my letter went to the wrong address, so it was several weeks before it reached the correct office. Senator Brown had a specific aid who handled veterans' affairs.

On Wednesday, September 27, Ms. Amber Moore called me personally. She apologized for the delay in responding to my earlier email. She said my letter went to the wrong office because Senator Brown has offices in Cleveland, Ohio, and Washington, D.C. Because of my email going to the wrong office, it took six weeks for my mail message to reach Senator Brown. Once he read my email, he contacted her and had her call me. I was surprised to be talking to an aide of a famous U.S. Senator.

Ms. Moore explained that she was the senator's aide who handled the veterans' issues. She explained that I needed to sign the privacy release form she sent and return it to her. Amber told me that Senator Brown would conduct a Congressional Inquiry on behalf of my father. The inquiry would see if any government agency would help pay for the cost of exhuming my father's remains and bringing him home. I was so grateful and amazed that someone in government cared enough to try to help me after six years of trying.

She asked me to fax her some documents and my story to her. She explained that Senator Brown would start the Congressional Inquiry once Senator Sherrod Brown received the documents. She also told me that such an inquiry would take some time. I was excited, so I grabbed the necessary papers and rushed to the Giant Eagle, where I worked, to fax them to Senator Brown's office.

Amber told me that a fire in 1973 fire destroyed my father's records. However, she said that their office would ask the researchers at the records office to search for other documents that could prove legal proof of military service. For the first time since I located my dad, I felt that my dream of meeting my dad would become a reality. She informed me that the research could take a few weeks because researchers would search through various government departments.

On March 9, 2017, I emailed the National Personnel Records Office in Saint Louis, Missouri, asking for help finding my father's military records. The following day the office replied, thanking me for sending my request. They asked for my signature so they could release the documents to me. I quickly went to Giant Eagle, where

I worked, and faxed over my signature.

On March 13, 2017, I received an email from the records office. They explained that they receive around 20,000 requests for military service records each week. They said that their goal was to reduce the response time to ten days or less.

On Thursday, April 6, I was given another position at my job. Besides being a cashier, I would be the backup to the file maintenance clerk. One of my duties was setting up the weekly sales for each week's ads and ensuring price accuracy.

The next day, the United States Department of Veterans Affairs informed me that they would send me the forms I would need to complete. Once I returned the documents, my father would be eligible for a headstone and American flag. It seemed like this year, God was answering my prayers to be reunited with my dad.

On Wednesday, April 12, 2017, I received a special package in the mail. The padded white envelope was from the National Personnel Records Office, so I knew what it was. It was an exciting moment because I knew it was the key to bringing my father and me together again.

At last, I held in my hands legal proof that my dad served in World War Two. The document had a government seal on it and was called a Certification of Military Service. For the first time in my life, I knew just how long my dad had served in the U.S. Army Air Force. He enlisted on April 4, 1942, and served through

November 30, 1945. For the first time in my life, I knew exactly how long my dad had served his country.

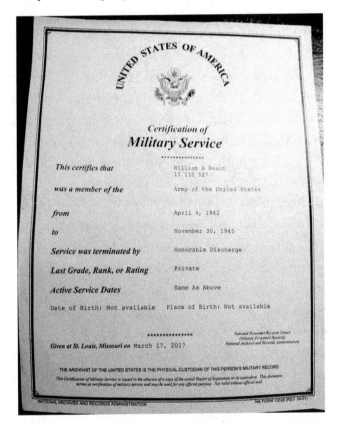

I quickly went out to a Dollar Tree store to buy a frame for my certificate to protect it. My spending money was limited, so I could not afford an expensive picture frame. Finally, I had the legal proof I needed to give my father the military funeral he deserved.

On April 13, 2017, I emailed a reporter from my town's newspaper, *The Canton Repository*. I told her about my father and how I was trying to bring his body back to Canton. I asked her if they would be interested in reporting about my father when I could get his remains home.

On April 14, Dave Sereno, one of the editors, emailed me to say that he would be interested in authoring a story about my father and me. He asked me to keep him informed as to my progress. For the following two months, I searched for more clues about my father after work in the evenings. Although I discovered my dad's military information, such facts were not legal proof for the government's burial benefits.

In June of 2017, I finally got approved for my first credit card since my divorce. I also learned that my credit score was over 700, which I knew was crucial to getting an unsecured personal bank loan. A bank loan officer explained that my debt-to-income ratio was too large because I still paid child support, so no bank would approve an unsecured loan for me. I was discouraged, so each day, from then on, I would listen to several different songs each evening on YouTube. The songs were "I Won't Back Down" by Tom Petty, "Overcomer" by Mandissa, "Don't Stop" by Fleetwood Mac, and "Shake" by Mercy Me.

Losing six weeks of work the year before because of my foot surgery made this year hard. I was just able to pay the rent and bills. I was saving up enough money to bury my father, but it seemed hopeless. I made a copy of the songs I listened to at night on a music compact disc. Each morning as I drove to work, I would listen to the songs. I would often listen to one music repeatedly, especially at night, when researching Ancestry. Certain lines from songs would encourage me not to give up on my dream.

On Saturday, July 15, 2017, I received my Medicare card in the mail. They informed me that in October, I would be able to apply for my social security benefits. I would be eligible for Social Security on my birthday on October 31, when I would turn 65. However, I would have to wait until the following February to receive my first check. I was still excited because I knew that in 2018 my income would increase each month by over fifty percent. This new income would allow me to reduce my debt-to-pay, to get a personal bank loan eventually. Then my dream of meeting my father would become a reality.

On August 8, 2017, I typed an email letter to Senator Sherrod Brown. The following day I received an automated response from Senator Brown's office. He thanked me for contacting him and told me that he would get back to me. I authored another email supplying more details about my father and the records I had found. Days turned into weeks, and I did not hear back from Senator Brown. I was discouraged, but I continued working full-time and searching for more clues about my dad online.

Besides finding more information about my father's ancestors, I spent September working and spending time with Sarah. I knew enough about how our government worked to see that it would take a while to hear from Senator Brown.

Although I could keep up with paying all my bills, most of my meals still consisted of bologna, hot dogs, and pasta. Except for when I was with my daughter, I rarely ate at a restaurant. I had to keep my goal of getting my finances in shape so that in 2018 I could get a bank loan for my dad. I was grateful for Senator Brown trying to help find money from the government to help. However, the past six years' experience gave me little hope.

Uncovering secrets

On October 1, 2017, I could file online to start receiving my social security checks beginning the following year. I took my social security a year before being fully vested, knowing that I would receive a slightly smaller monthly payment. I did so because I learned that I could still work full-time at Giant Eagle and collect Social Security the year before reaching full retirement age. Even though I was still struggling to have enough money to buy gas, I felt hopeful that 2018 would be the year I finally would meet my dad.

I also emailed Dave Sereno from the *Canton Repository* to update him on my progress on bringing my dad home. I told him that I faxed Senator Sherrod Brown the necessary documents about my father to begin a Congressional Inquiry the week before. The inquiry was to find a way to pay for the cost of exhuming my father and returning his remains.

I informed Mr. Sereno that I had found evidence

that my mother had been married to someone else before meeting my dad. After my mother died from dementia in 2006, I found her original discharge papers from the U.S. Navy in 1945. It showed her last name as Phillips. I also found two old photos of her with her first husband, dating back to World War 2. After some time researching Ancestry, I learned that my mother married a Newell Phillips on May 22, 1937. According to a 1940 census, my mother had a son named either Braley or Bradley.

It was quite a revelation to discover that not only had my mother been married before, but that she had had a son that she had kept a secret all my life. Even more impressive was the fact that my mother and her first husband grew up just several miles from each other. I also found evidence that my mother's first husband's relatives lived in the same area as my mother's relatives throughout my childhood. I was amazed at how well my mother and all my relatives could keep such secrets all their lives.

On Saturday, October 21, 2017, I received a letter from Senator Sherrod Brown. He informed me that the Department of Veterans Affairs would not pay for the cost of disinterment. They also told Senator Brown that they would not cover transporting my father's body back to Ohio. I also learned a National Cemetery in Dallas, Texas, could bury my father. However, it would cost me around $5,000 to exhume his remains and move them to that cemetery. I decided that even if I were to go into debt, I would bring my dad back to Ohio.

I updated Mr. Sereno from the *Canton Repository* about my setback. I also told him that I had read articles online that the Pentagon spent 294 million dollars between 2011 and 2015 on medications like Viagra. However, our government will not spend a dime to honor a fallen hero of World War II. That day, I was discouraged, and I told Mr. Sereno that I might not live long enough to be reunited with my father. I told him that I would keep trying, however. I mentioned a line from a Tom Petty song that I often listened to, which encouraged me. I said that I would stand my ground and not back down.

On Monday, November 20, I received a large brown envelope in the mail. Inside was an official Presidential Memorial Certificate from President Donald Trump. It had the presidential seal stamped in gold, and President Trump had signed it. I was immensely proud of my dad and that he was finally getting the recognition he deserved. I quickly took a photo of the certificate and posted it to my friends on Facebook.

I assumed that this was due to the Congressional Inquiry Senator Brown had conducted. That evening I emailed the White House. I thanked them for the certificate. I also asked them if they could help with the financial cost of returning my father's body to Ohio. I also suggested that President Trump would be one of the pallbearers.

To my surprise, the following day, I received an email from the Office of Presidential Correspondence. One of the staff wrote that the White House staff had read my letter and had sent it to another federal agency for further action. I realized that the President had not read my request, and I never heard back from any other agency. I was disappointed, but I refused to give up hope.

On November 24, I emailed Mr. Sereno to update him about my progress with my father. I told him that in October, Senator Sherrod Brown conducted a Congressional Inquiry about my father. Unfortunately, no government agency would help pay for the cost of exhuming or transporting my father. I also told him about the Presidential Memorial Certificate I recently received in the mail. The following day he replied to thank me for keeping him updated and to say he was still interested in my story.

Birthdays

On Tuesday, November 27, I was informed by the Social Security Administration that I would receive my first social security check on February 2, 2018. A member of the administration explained that since my full retirement age was in 2018, I could still work full time while collecting my benefits. The extra income was the key to my plan to bring my dad home.

On January 1, 2011, my oldest daughter, Ashley, had turned eighteen and no longer needed child support. Now she was 25 and working at a local Subway restaurant.

I set a goal to start 2018 by paying down more of my outstanding bills like credit cards, so my credit score would increase. Doing that would also improve my debt-to-income ratio and was also crucial in ever getting a personal bank loan.

I spent December working and spending every other weekend with Sarah. I could not find any government agency to help me financially to bring my father home. I decided to get approved one day in 2018 for an unsecured personal loan by a bank.

In my research on my dad, I had discovered that he was the first cousin, four times removed of Elizabeth Anne Beach. She married William Samuel Johnson, who played a crucial role in creating our Constitution. I mentioned this fact in my emails to several members of our government. I hoped that it might help me to get some financial aid.

Unfortunately, it did not make any difference. On Saturday, December 4th, I emailed Senator Brown to thank him for trying to find financial help from our government. I shared that I had tried writing the White House but received no support. I told him that he could be one of the pallbearers when I eventually brought my dad home.

On January 1, 2018, my oldest daughter Ashley turned 25. For Ashley and Sarah's birthdays, I would take them to a local Mexican restaurant. It was sort of a tradition that we did for each of our birthdays. After our meals, the staff came to our table to sing happy birthday to whichever one had a birthday.

I believed that this year would be the year I would get a bank loan to bring my father back home. Although I knew that my monthly income would increase in February, I had little money after paying all my monthly bills in January. I had planned to take both of my daughters to Olive Garden on January 6 to celebrate Ashley turning 25 and Sarah turning sweet

16 on January 8.

The Sunday before, I shared with my friends in Sunday School what I wanted to do. They were aware of my financial situation, and one couple gave me some money to help me pay for my daughters' meals. The day came when I took Ashley and Sarah out to Olive Garden. To make sure I had enough money, I had to use some of the Kennedy half dollars that I had saved since I was a teenager. We had a wonderful time together, and afterward, I went back to my home alone.

Accident at work

On Tuesday, January 23, I had an unusual accident at my workplace. I was in the lobby, cleaning a shelf. As I started to walk away, another employee passed by pushing some shopping carts. I was caught off-balance and fell flat on my face breaking my glasses. As I rolled over on my back, I felt pain and saw that I was bleeding. A coworker who saw me fall reported my fall to customer service. They called for a store responder who was responsible for the management of an accident. Several managers and coworkers came to check on me. One friend commented that I must not be hurt too badly because I was making jokes.

A member of management drove me to a local emergency room. After a brain scan and tetanus shot, a doctor told me that they had found some fluid buildup on the right side of my brain. He said it looked like it was not related to my fall and was not dangerous. A manager came to return me to work, but before going back to work, I had to go to another medical center.

Upon arrival at the next clinic, I met a nurse. She told me that I had to take a drug and alcohol test since I had a work injury. I had trouble accepting the breathalyzer test for alcohol. A nurse wanted me to take a deep breath and exhale into a tube on the machine. I could not make her understand that it hurt to inhale because of my accident. Finally, another nurse came in and showed her how to help me take the test. Once I passed the two tests, I could leave. I went back to work, and then I drove home to rest and take a couple of days off. It took a couple of weeks for the bruise on my right eye to fade away.

Progress at last

In the first week of February, I received my first social security check. I felt a deep sense of relief. For the first time in nine years, I had enough money for extra things like eating out or buying new clothes. I knew I could go and buy something, but I focused on paying down my debt. I knew that the only way to bring my dad home was to get an unsecured bank loan. Although my credit score was improving, I also had to lower my debt-to-income more. This month was a game changer for me.

I also learned that they would pay the monthly child support for my daughter Sarah until she became an adult at age eighteen. My social security payment each month to my daughter Sarah would be double that taken from my paycheck. I notified my local child support agency, and they ruled that my social security was now child support. The result was that now my monthly income would almost double. Like a runner in a marathon, I was near the finish line, in my case the point of getting a bank loan to bring my dad home.

Later in February, I had an eye exam to get new glasses to replace the damaged ones in my fall at work. The doctor told me that I had a small cataract forming in both of my eyes. He told me that they could grow at different rates, but he could not operate on my eyes at the time.

As February ended, I called the Social Security Administration. I spoke to an agent, and I asked them to give me my father's work history. An agent told me that I needed to send them a payment and legal proof I was his son. Then he told me they would send me my father's entire work history. I acted quickly and faxed the necessary documents to prove I was his son. I learned it would take a few weeks to get my report. I was hoping to find a business where my dad had worked and information about him. I was hopeful that my dad had worked for many years at a company and had a life insurance policy. I hoped that maybe I could find a way to pay for his burial.

In March, the movie *I Can Only Imagine* came out in theaters. I watched it several times because it reminded me of my childhood. In the film, Bart Millard's mother left when he was young, and his father was verbally critical of him as he grew up. In my case, my father left, and my mother was verbally abusive to me. Later in life, Bart Millard's dad became a Christian, and they reconciled. Bart Millard honored his dad by writing a song. The movie encouraged me to keep trying to honor my father by giving him the burial he deserved.

On April 24, 2018, the check I had mailed to the Social Security Administration two months earlier was processed. I was encouraged because that meant that soon I would receive my father's work history.

On May 5, while researching Ancestry, I finally found more evidence about my mother's first husband. I found a newspaper obituary for a Newell Wendel Phillips. He died on December 10, 2011, in a town near Cleveland, Ohio. There was a photo of him from when he served in World War 2. I compared it to the ones I had of my mother and a man, and they looked a lot alike. His date of birth matched as well as the area where he grew up.

I wondered why my mother's relatives were all able to keep so many secrets hidden for over half a century.

During May, I also traced my father's ancestors back to the fourteenth century. During that time, my father's ancestors lived in Aldsworth, England. Then their last name was De La Beche, and nine of them were knights over seven feet tall.

I decided to research my ancestors online. I learned that some of my ancestors were either members of the Kin's guards of the Tower of London or sheriffs of towns in southern England. They served both King Edward II and King Edward III. The De La Beche family also had their own castle in a small village called Aldsworth. In a church, there reside nine life-size statues of the De La Beche family. I rather fancied having a last name of De La Beche.

While I waited to receive my father's work history, I checked my credit score and found out that it was getting better. I became confident that this would be the year I would meet my dad.

In June, I heard about the Patriot Guard Riders and how they supplied a motorcycle escort for veterans' funerals. I watched YouTube videos that showed the Patriot Guard Riders escorting a hearse through towns. I decided that I would like to do that for my father if it were possible.

On the evening of July 7, I was searching online. I discovered a free genealogical website called Famous Kin. There I was able to type in any name of one of my ancestors. In less than a minute, their search engine listed any famous people your ancestor is related to.

I discovered that I was the first cousin eight times removed to Warren Buffett, a famous businessman. I had trouble breathing for a few seconds because I found out my sixth-great-aunt was the sister to Warren Buffet's seventh-great-grandfather. I like genealogy most because it shows how important each of us is and how our decisions can influence the future.

A couple of days later, I discovered that I was the first cousin eight times removed to the famous actor Christopher Lloyd of the *Back to the Future* movies. I printed out a copy of a photo of him on my printer. I took it to work the next day and told my friends that I was a distant first cousin. Several friends told me that I looked just like him, and one friend thought he was my dad. I decided to write a letter to Christopher

Lloyd and introduce myself and my daughters to him. I typed a letter to him explaining how we were related. I also included a photo of my daughters and me. Unfortunately, I never received a reply.

I was also excited to discover that my father was the third cousin two times removed to Princess Diana. As time went on, I would find out that my family was related to many famous people throughout history.

The journey home begins

Although I had enough proof to bring my father's body home, I still could not do so because of the financial cost. I was able to collect social security starting in February and still work full-time at Giant Eagle. I then continued to focus on paying down my debts and increasing my credit score.

On July 13, 2018, I decided to get a personal loan from a bank. I had tried several times the previous two years. Unfortunately, the rules for getting approved for an unsecured private bank loan are stringent. I went to a Citizen's Bank office near where I lived and completed the application for an unsecured bank loan. I explained that my request was to use the money to bury my father.

The loan officer put all my information into her computer. After just a few minutes, she told me that I was pre-approved for a $10,000 personal loan. The loan officer told me it would be several days before knowing whether the bank had approved my loan. Still, she believed that there would be no problem.

I was thrilled that I would finally have the money to bring my father's body home. I searched for a funeral director in Grand Prairie, Texas. I contacted Mark Dean, the co-owner of the Guerrero-Dean Funeral Home. I explained my situation, and he agreed to help me. Mr. Dean explained that the paperwork would take a couple of months to process. He explained to me how he would disinter my father and transport his remains.

I learned that a Dallas County Medical Examiner would work with him in exhuming my father. As much as I wished I could be at the gravesite that day, Mr. Dean said it would be best if I were not there, as the exhumation could be disturbing to anyone not used to such a thing. My dad had been placed inside a grave with a concrete liner with a concrete slab on top, and he explained that part of my father's body might be more than bones.

After talking with Mr. Dean, I decided to have my father's remains returned in a coffin. He explained that he would have to use a special metal coffin that would be sealed. The airlines required this special coffin because my father's remains were more than bones. A sealed casket was needed to prevent any smells from escaping.

I learned that a medical examiner would have to open the body bag to confirm they had the right body. I decided it would be best not to watch that process.

I missed my dad so much that I wanted to be there the moment they exhumed him. However, I realized it would be best to remember him from my photo of him and not from how he looked after two decades in the grave.

On Monday, July 16, the bank let me know that the bank had approved my loan request. I was both thrilled and excited. Two days later, on Wednesday evening, I decided to call one of the North Texas Patriot Guards' board members, Brenda Rowell. I explained my situation and asked for her help. She told me that she would contact the captain who oversaw the riders near the cemetery.

A couple of days later, a member of the North Texas Patriot Guard Riders called me. He said they would investigate escorting my father's body from the funeral home in Grand Prairie, Texas, to Canton, Ohio.

The following evening, I emailed the secretary of the National Board of the Patriot Guard Riders. I explained my situation, and she replied that they could help. She explained that I would need to fax them a copy of my father's military service certificate. I mentioned that I had decided to have my father returned in a special metal coffin.

On July 26, my funeral director from Texas faxed me the forms I needed to sign to exhume my father. I signed them and faxed them back to him when I was at work. Mr. Dean told me that it would take around six to eight weeks before the Dallas County Medical Examiner's Office would process my quest.

He explained that the city of Dallas had never seen my type of the request before. I was disappointed that it would take so long, but I understood that doing things with the government takes time.

I was curious, so I did some research on the city of Dallas, Texas. In 2018 the town had 1.345 million people. I wondered how I could be the first person ever to try to find a missing person and then exhume them and move them.

I had a couple of friends wonder why I would do all this and go into debt for a father who deserted me. I told them that I knew that he had loved me from the one photo I had of my dad and me. I also said that my dad fought in World War 2, which meant that he deserved a proper burial.

The following day I emailed the editor of the *Canton Repository*. I updated him on my progress with my father and told him that I wanted to have the Patriot Guard Riders escort my father's casket down through the town. He was interested in taking photos of them along with a story. I still had the impression that I would be able to bring my dad home sometime in September.

Two days after this, I sent an email to Channel 19 News in Cleveland, Ohio. Now that I knew for sure my dad was coming home, I wanted to let the local press know in hopes that they would do a story about my father.

On Friday, August 3, Mr. Dean told me that he could find me a casket that would not cost much more than the cost of having my father's remains returned in an urn. I was glad to be able to get a casket for my father that would fit my budget. He explained that the coffin cost would be around $1,500, and the cost of a plane trip from Dallas, Texas, to Cleveland, Ohio, would be about $300.00.

On August 6, I posted to Facebook about my dad. I wrote that at 7:50 pm, August 6, 1999, my father drew his last breath at Baylor University Hospital in Dallas, Texas. Even though I had not been around my father for over six decades, the thought of him dying alone with not even one friend nearby made me sad. I told my friends that I wished I could travel back in time to the day my dad passed away to hold his hand and say that I loved him just before he died.

On Thursday, August 16, 2018, I emailed a news station in Grand Prairie, Texas. I told them about my father and that I was planning to return his remains to my hometown. Later that day, a news reporter, Bob Fitch, replied to my email. I told him that I believed that a funeral director would exhume my father sometime in September. He told me that he would cover my father's exhumation and return, which made me very happy.

I spent the following two weeks either working or spending time with Sarah. I did not receive any more information from my funeral director in Texas during this time.

One evening, while researching Ancestry.com, I came across a news article about another forgotten person in Southland Memorial Park. In 1999, the cemetery had buried a woman named Lee Lozano in an unmarked grave like my father. She was a well-known artist in New York but decided to stop painting and went to Dallas, Texas, in 1982.

When she died a couple of months after my father died, the cemetery also buried her in an unmarked grave. In 2016 some of her artwork was discovered and began to sell for a half-million dollars each. Ms. Lozano remained in an unmarked grave because no one claimed her body.

On Wednesday, September 5, I received an email from Mr. Dean in Grand Prairie, Texas. He told me that he still had not heard anything from Dallas's city about granting the permit to exhume my father. He said he would work with the national cemetery and my funeral director in Ohio to make the arrangements.

Mr. Dean mentioned that it could be possible to have the Patriot Guard Riders escort my father's casket by land. However, the cost would be around $3,600. That figure would not include the cost of having my father kept at a funeral home overnight during the trip. I had seen videos on YouTube of the Patriot Guard Riders escorting veterans' remains. Watching all the motorcycles with their flags flying was very moving to me. However, I realized that I only had so much money. This would raise the cost by a couple of thousand dollars more than my loan, so I decided to stay with the plan of returning my father's body by airplane. Mr. Dean explained that he would get back to me about the flight's total cost once he received the permit from Dallas's city.

As each day went by, I felt anxious. Since the Dallas County Medical Examiner had never seen a request like mine, I worried they might deny my claim. My funeral director told me that the city could only reject my application if my father was dishonorably discharged or convicted of capital murder.

I knew that I could save thousands of dollars by just having a headstone on the grave where my dad was. However, I could not stand the thought of him not being in a casket, and I wanted the chance to touch his coffin and give him a proper burial. The fact that I believed he had deserted me was irrelevant. I knew from the one photo I had of us together that my dad loved me. I would not exist without him, so I was determined to see him get a military burial.

In the middle of September, my company decided to grant me three days of paid bereavement leave. My manager told me that I could use my paid days off work when I could finally bring my father back home. It took a while for the decision to be made because I was the first employee to ask for such leave twenty years after the death first occurred.

Although I still had not received a permit to exhume my father, I decided to look for a funeral home in my town for help. The first funeral home I went to was lovely but expensive. The funeral director told me that I could save money by just driving to Texas and putting my father's casket in the back of a pickup truck. Then

I could go home myself and save on transportation costs. I was not sure if he was joking, but I decided to look elsewhere.

I decided to check with the Rossi Funeral Home, which was close to the church I attended. I emailed the director, and he responded quickly. He explained in detail what was needed to bury my father at our national cemetery. He even emailed me a detailed list of the charges for his services, which impressed me.

On the last weekend of September, I told the funeral director I would accept his services. I gave him the phone number of my funeral director in Grand Prairie, Texas, and a copy of my dad's military service certificate.

On October 3, I decided to make out a will online through a company's program. Since I had been dealing with my father's burial, I had begun to think about my future. I decided to write a new will since the one I made while married was not updated.

The middle of October marked three months since my funeral director in Texas had applied for a permit with the Dallas County Medical Examiner. I emailed him expressing my frustration, and he explained that he could only wait for the decision. He assured me that he would arrange the details with Patriot Guard Riders and the airplane flight once he got the permit.

The rest of October was uneventful except for turning 66 on October 31. I had my birthday off because I worked overnight. However, I was able to dress up as "Doc Brown" the day before. When I went to work that night, my coworkers gave me a cake and sang happy birthday, which was a pleasant surprise.

On Monday, November 12, I was driving home from work, and I noticed a traffic jam near an exit that led to my home. The traffic on the interstate slowly came to a complete stop. I had just turned on my emergency lights when the car behind me struck me from behind. The driver had stopped behind me, but the woman behind her was distracted and hit her.

Once again, my Chevy Impala had kept me safe, and I was able to drive home once the traffic was clear. The state trooper who took my statement had to stand on the driver's side because the oncoming traffic would not slow down. I was able to drive home. The following day I received a rental car so that a car repair shop could install a new rear bumper.

Breakthrough

Two days later, I emailed the *Canton Repository* editor to update him about my father's progress. I told him that the Dallas County Medical Examiner still had not approved my permit. I explained that as soon as I learned anything, I would let him know.

On Thursday, November 15, after I got home from work, I emailed Senator Sherrod Brown. I explained that it was now four months since I had applied for a permit to return my father's body to Ohio. I asked Senator Brown to help in some way. I explained that the officials in Dallas, Texas, needed to release my father's body so I could bury him in Western Reserve National Cemetery. To my surprise, the following morning, I received an email from him. I was amazed that it was dated at 5:21 am. Senator Brown thanked me for contacting him and said that he would investigate the matter.

On Tuesday, November 20, I was at work when I

went into an office. I was getting ready to print out several sale signs when I received a phone call from Amber, the aide who handled veterans' affairs for Senator Brown. She told me that they had contacted the officials in the State of Texas, and they were waiting to hear back from them. She also explained that she could help with a headstone for my father. I was thrilled to listen to some good news for a change.

Amber also told me that Senator Brown would have an American flag flown over the United States Capitol to honor my father's military service. She explained that it would happen around the date of my father's burial. After she ended the call, I placed my phone down on the table. The thought that my father would go from being forgotten in an unmarked grave to having an American flag flown over our nation's capital was overwhelming. I put my face in my hands and began crying. I wanted to go back to work, but I could not stop crying. After a half-hour had passed, I was able to compose myself and return to work.

That evening I emailed Mr. Dean in Texas to let him know that Senator Sherrod Brown was looking into the matter. He replied and told me that he had called the State Office of Vital Statistics the day before. They told him they had the application and my payment for the exhumation of my father's body.

They still would not say when they would say yes, even after four months had passed. I was frustrated, but I believed that now something would happen soon.

Seven days after Senator Brown's aides contacted

the officials in Dallas, Texas, I learned from his office that the Dallas County Medical Examiner had approved the disinterment.

I was thrilled that the state of Texas had finally approved the paperwork to my funeral director in Texas. Mr. Dean emailed me with the cost of everything, including the plane flight home. Then I contacted my funeral director in Canton to let him know that I got the permit. We decided to meet a few days later to discuss plans and so I could give him the documents our national cemetery needed to approve my father's burial. Since I had the days off from work, I also emailed the *Canton Repository* editor to tell him the good news that I got the permit.

Before I met with my funeral director in town, I talked with my director in Texas. He recommended against trying to return my father in December because of the holidays. He recommended sometime in early January. I understood the logic, but I was eager to be with my dad again. I had dreamed for months of having the Ohio Patriot Guard Riders escort my father's hearse through the streets of Canton. I had pictured people lined along the roads, paying tribute to him, as I had seen in YouTube videos. It was December now, and I realized those dreams would not come true.

On Friday, December 1, I met with my funeral director in town. We agreed on a tentative date of either January 9 or 10 for my father's burial at the Western Reserve National Cemetery. The exact date would depend on when his plane would land here in Ohio and at which airport. That evening I emailed the captain of the North Texas Patriot Guard Riders. I told him about my plans, and he told me they would escort my father's casket to the Dallas Fort Worth International Airport. That weekend I informed Pastor Dan Hanson from my church about my plans. Dan suggested that it would be best to have the funeral and burial on the same day.

Interviews

On Sunday evening, December 2, 2018, I authored an email to Pam Cook, News/Talk 1480 WHBT radio news director in my town. I shared with her my father's story. I was just hoping that their radio station would cover my father's return to Canton, Ohio.

The following day Ms. Cook replied and said she was forwarding my email to the Saturday morning host, Joe Palmisano. She explained that he might contact me and that she thought my story was beautiful.

On Monday, my funeral director in Canton tried to call Western Reserve National Cemetery's office to schedule my father's burial. Still, they were closed because former President George H.W. Bush had recently passed away. On Wednesday afternoon, I was driving my daughter Sarah home from her school in Hartville, Ohio. My phone rang, and I answered even though I did not recognize the phone number.

I was so amazed to hear Joe Palmisano talking

to me that I almost dropped my phone. He told me that Pam Cook had shared my story with him. Then Joe asked me if I would be willing to do a live radio interview with him in three days, on Saturday. For a few seconds, I was speechless because I was talking to a radio personality. I told Joe that I would be willing to do the interview.

On December 6, 2018, at 10:30 am, the National Cemetery Scheduling Office contacted me. They informed me that my dad was approved for burial at the Western Reserve National Cemetery on Thursday, January 10, 2019, at 2 pm. A member of the staff told me they would bury my father with full military honors. I felt relieved to know that my funeral director had the time and date set for my father's burial.

I was disappointed that the weather would be cold, but I accepted that it was the best I could do. I could wait until it was warm weather where I lived, but I did not want to wait a few more months. It had already been five months since I first applied for a permit. That evening I emailed Bob Fitch of the *Grand Prairie Reporter*. I informed him that the national cemetery had set a date for my father's burial. He agreed to take photos and report on my father in his town in Texas.

The following day Mr. Sereno from the *Canton Repository* emailed me. He asked if I would be willing to speak with one of his reporters. I replied that I would be ready, and I told him about the details I had for my father's funeral and burial.

The following day Shane Hoover from the *Canton*

Repository emailed me. He asked me if he could interview me the next week for a story.

I replied, and we agreed on a time on Wednesday, December 12. I arranged to meet him at the cafe in Giant Eagle, where I worked. He asked me to bring my father's work history and documents to have more details for his news article.

Friday, December 7, 2018, was an eventful day for me. When I was on a break at work, Amber called me. She told me that the Senator would try to make it to my father's funeral. If his schedule would not allow him to come, Ms. Moore said she would stand in for him.

I spent the evening getting ready for my live interview with Joe Palmisano Saturday morning. I was nervous because I was unsure if he would hear me and speak loud enough.

On December 8, 2018, I awoke and got ready for my live interview. At 10 am, I received a phone call from Joe Palmisano. He told me that he was getting prepared for my interview and that I just needed to leave my phone connected. I placed my phone on my computer desk in my living room and got ready for the interview. I could hear Joe talking on his radio program at the station. I heard him announce to his audience that after a commercial, he would interview me.

I sat at my desk and listened to Joe describe my story as incredible and unique just before he started to talk to me. I was nervous because I am often soft-spoken, and I wondered if the audience would hear me. As Joe began to interview me, I was surprised to find myself talking to him as comfortably as if he was in my living room. I shared my story about my father, and our interview went on for about a half-hour. There was a commercial break midway through our discussion, so I posted on Facebook that I was doing a live interview with Joe. I was excited and glad that a radio personality was impressed by my father's story. After our discussion, Joe thanked me for talking with him, and we hung up.

After I hung up my phone, I felt my body shaking because I was so excited to have completed a live interview. I posted on Facebook about my talk and that my father's casket would arrive in Cleveland the following week. I told my friends that I felt like Indiana Jones and that the casket carrying my father was like the Ark of the Covenant. I did not just want to touch the container but the casket inside, which was a treasure. One friend who heard my interview did not realize it was me. She told me she was surprised it was me because I spoke with clarity and articulation.

On Tuesday, December 11, I was at work, and I went into the file maintenance clerk's office. I was getting ready to print several sale signs, and I laid my cell phone on the table by my computer. Before I could do anything, I received a phone call. It was from Senator Brown's office. Amber wanted to tell me that the senator would not make it to my father's funeral or burial but that she would come in his place. Before she hung up, she informed me that Senator Brown would have an American flag flown over the U.S. Capitol Building one day in January.

More interviews

On Wednesday morning, December 12, 2018, I got dressed and prepared to go to Giant Eagle, where I worked. I got ready to go to the cafe to meet with a news reporter from the *Canton Repository*. I gathered the relevant documents about my father, like proof of his military service.

When I entered the cafe at work at 10 am, Mr. Hoover was already there. He introduced himself, and then we sat down at a long table. Just then, my store manager walked past us. I wondered if he thought I was being interviewed for another job, because I had many documents.

I felt calm, even though this was my first in-person interview. I shared my story about my father and my nine-year struggle to find him and be reunited. Mr. Hoover then asked to look at my father's work history from the Social Security Administration. He started to look over all the sheets. Several times I heard him say, "wow." He seemed amazed that my dad had worked eighty-six jobs in sixteen states, from California to Ohio. I was surprised when after my interview, Mr. Hoover asked me to make copies of every page of my father's work history. He also took pictures of the documents I brought. I was impressed by his professionalism.

On Thursday, I received a phone call from the press secretary for U.S. Senator Sherrod Brown. I was surprised to think that I was that important. He explained that reporters wanted to ask the senator about me and my story. Still, I had to give their office permission before they could talk to reporters. I learned that anyone who receives help from a Congress member has their privacy protected unless they give their permission for their story to be told to the press. I felt like somebody important, which was a feeling I had not felt until recently.

That evening I emailed my funeral director in Texas. I informed him that the National Cemetery Scheduling Office had approved my father's burial with full military honors the previous Thursday. It was set for 2 pm at Western Reserve National Cemetery.

On Friday, December 14, 2019, Mr. Hoover sent me an email and planned to meet me the following Friday at my home. He told me that he would bring a camera operator to take pictures of my father's documents. He also said to me that the newspaper would do an article about my father and me. After reading his email, I was excited, and I did not realize that my story would soon be front-page news.

I also received an email that day from a staff member from Channel 19 News in Cleveland, Ohio. They told me that they had received my story about my father and wanted to interview me on camera at their studios in Cleveland in a few days. Over the weekend, I emailed my father's story to *Inside Edition* producers, but they never responded. I wanted to tell the entire world about my father.

Tuesday, December 18, became one of the most exciting days of my life. It started when I received an email from a reporter from Channel 19 news. She told me that they wanted to interview me at their studios on December 26, right after Christmas. She told me to bring my father's documents with me and be at their studios at 11:30 am. I was both excited and nervous. While I felt comfortable talking to a reporter, doing so in front of cameras would be a new experience.

Later that afternoon, I went to a T.J. Max department store to buy a new pair of pants for my future interviews. I was in line with my youngest daughter, Sarah, when my phone rang. I did not recognize the number, but I decided to answer it. I was so surprised to hear it was a news reporter from the *Cleveland Plain Dealer* that I almost dropped my phone. He told me that he wanted to interview me on December 27 at my home for an article in their newspaper. I told him I would do the interview.

I paid for my clothes and went to my car to take Sarah back home to her mother. However, I had to wait a few minutes because I had trouble catching my breath. Several friends and my ex-wife told me that I was a celebrity. I felt somewhat overwhelmed because I would meet my dad finally in a few days, plus all the notoriety was overwhelming. However, sometimes I would experience pain and sorrow when I thought about how my father died alone and was buried only in a body bag.

I spent the evening getting ready for my interview and photoshoot the next day with Shane Hoover and the *Canton Repository* photographer. I received a video chat on my phone from a friend. He told me that I looked ten years younger and had a kind of glow on my face. After many years of struggling to bring my dad home, I guess the media attention gave me the excitement I never thought I would feel. Each day there were moments that I would think about my father and feel grief over his being buried all alone. However, there were other times when I felt like I could bend steel in my bare hands.

At 11 am on December 19, Shane Hoover and the photographer came to my home for the interview. I had on the only nice shirt I had, which was a purple one. I wore a tie since they wanted a photo for the newspaper. The photographer had a large camera with lenses, so I could tell he was a professional. He took several pictures, including one of me sitting at my desk, holding the only photo of my dad and me, and the only one of my parents.

Shane told me before they left that my story would be in the newspaper that Sunday. He also said that they were considering putting my account on their front page if nothing significant happened before then. After they left, I was delighted and excited.

Later that day, the funeral director from Grand Prairie, Texas, sent me an email. He assured me that my father's remains would arrive in time for the funeral. When the cemetery buried my father in 1999, they had placed him in a body bag, with a tag around his foot with his details. They did that so that if someone tried to claim his remains, they would have an identification.

Mark Dean also told me that after the cemetery buried my dad, they placed a small spike with a flat disc on top of the ground. It had a case number on it to identify the grave. He said that the grass might have grown over it after so many years, but he had a unique tool to find the marker. It hurt me to know that my dad had no headstone.

On Thursday, December 20, 2018, I worked overnight at Giant Eagle. I spent the night making signs and getting the store ready for the next weekly sale. After I got off work, I drove back to my home. A reporter from the *Cleveland Plain Dealer*, Mr. Albrecht, had planned to interview me that morning. I went upstairs to get a shower and get ready for my interview.

I had just enough time to make some coffee to keep me going. I was sleepy, but I did not want to miss the chance to share my story with another reporter. I was not aware at first that I would be videotaped by Mr. Albrecht, so I dressed casually. A few minutes before my interview, I received an email from my ex-wife. She informed me that neither of my daughters would attend my father's funeral service or burial. I was saddened but not surprised. I shook it off and prepared myself for my interview.

I had to share a driveway with a neighbor who thought she owned the driveway. I decided it would be best for Mr. Albrecht to park on the street and walk down the driveway to my home. I thought I would just share my story, but Brian also set up a small camera to record my interview. I learned a part of my interview would appear on the newspaper's website.

I was relaxed and not nervous that he was videotaping me. He used a cell phone on top of a tripod to record a video of my interview. I shared my story and included how Christopher Lloyd influenced my life. When he asked me what family members would be attending my father's funeral service, I told him only my father. He seemed very surprised.

Since I had mentioned *Back to The Future* to him, he then asked me would I go back to the past to stop my parents from breaking up if I could. I replied that I could not, even if it meant I could have a normal childhood. I explained that if I did that, my oldest daughter, Ashley, would not have had a Christian education, and my youngest daughter, Sarah, would not have been born.

Mr. Albrecht took photos of my father's documents as proof of military service. My interview lasted for about an hour. When Brian finished his talk, I thanked him and said goodbye. It took a while to relax enough to sleep because I found the interview to be extremely exciting.

On Friday, December 21, Mr. Sereno from the *Canton Repository* sent me an email. He told me that they would print the story about my father and me one day before Christmas. I was thrilled and anxious to see what the article would say.

On Sunday, December 23, I went to work at Giant Eagle at 9 AM. I quickly went to the newspaper stand and saw my story had made the *Canton Repository*'s front page. I was even more excited to see that a color photo of me holding pictures of my parents was also on the front page. I bought several copies. I also told my co-workers and customers throughout the day. Several friends called me a celebrity.

A mystery revealed

~

On Sunday, December 23, 2018, I went to work at Giant Eagle in the morning. It was fascinating to me to see myself on the front page of the *Canton Repository*. There was a two-page article about my search for my father. It included the only photo of my dad and me when I was a baby. I bought several copies to keep and give to my daughters.

Customers were quite surprised to see that I was on the front page of the newspaper. I told my customers about my dad as I rang up their orders. In the evening, I told my friends on Facebook that I wished God would let me go back in time to August 6, 1999, to be by my dad's side before he died, hold his hand and tell him that I loved him.

The following evening was Christmas Eve. I was alone at home after working during the day. I thought about my father, and I decided to look through my father's work history from the Social Security

Administration months earlier. I looked closely at the eighty-six jobs my father had held over sixty years. I discovered something that I had not noticed before.

My mother had always led me to believe that my father ran away when I was around two years old. However, I noticed that my father had worked in Dayton, Ohio, until 1958. It seemed odd that my dad would run away from my mother and me when I was around two and yet work in the same town.

Then I remembered some of the old photos of my mother and me when I was little. I remembered that my mother told me she would leave me at her parents' home when she worked after my dad was gone. They lived in a small town called Stewartsville, which was near the West Virginia border of Ohio. Long forgotten memories returned as I thought more about my past. I remembered growing up, my mother telling me she had to live in a couple of different small towns near where she grew up before I reached school age.

Then I realized that my father had worked at jobs from one end of the country to another. For the first time in my life, it dawned on me that it was my mother who had run away. All the secrecy of my mother and her relatives about my father and his family now made sense. They would never want me to know that it was my mother who had run away in 1954 by kidnapping me. I wondered then if the real reason my dad had worked so many different jobs was that he had hoped to find me someday. I knew I might never know for sure which of my parents had left the other.

The day after Christmas, I woke up early. I gathered the documents and photos of my father. I had to leave early enough to get to the Channel 19 Studios in Cleveland for my interview.

Since it was the day after Christmas, the streets were not too busy. I found a parking spot near the studio. I felt like I was in Hollywood, even though I knew I was in Cleveland. I dressed casually but brought my shirt and tie. After I went inside, I met the receptionist. Then, Dan DeRoos met me in the lobby and escorted me to the room to interview me.

As I followed him, I saw the Channel 19 newsroom with the rows of reporters to my right. I felt like I was inside the *Daily Planet* from the original *Superman* movie. I was too excited to be nervous about my interview.

Dan DeRoss led me into a studio that looked just like the studios I had seen while watching the news. I made my way to the place where I was to sit. I was a little nervous when I saw the cinematographer and his large camera. While I had done interviews before, this was the first one inside an actual news studio. The cameraman took photos of the documents about my dad.

Then Dan DeRoss began our interview. I suggested dressing up, but he said it was okay for me to dress casually like I was. Once we started talking, I forgot about the camera not far in front of me. Our interview ended around 12:15 pm, and then Dan DeRoss escorted me out to my car. He told me that the station would televise his talk that day during the first ten minutes of Channel 19 News at 5 pm. He told me that he was amazed by my story, which made me feel good inside.

I drove home incredibly happy. When I got home, my funeral director in Texas had emailed me. I learned that the Dallas County Medical Examiner's office still had not set a date to dig up my father's body to be returned to Ohio.

Preparing for the journey home

The following day, on December 27, Mr. Dean emailed me from Grand Prairie, Texas. He gave me the details on how he would return my dad. The date for my father's disinterment was set for January 8, 2019, at 5 am. The following day at 8:30 am, the Texas Patriot Guard Riders would escort my father's hearse from Grand Prairie, Texas, to the Dallas Fort Worth International Airport.

Then at 11:05 am, American Airlines flight #1541 would take off for the Cleveland Hopkins International Airport. The expected arrival was 2:43 pm. Mr. Dean also gave me the authorization forms that I needed to sign and fax back to him. I printed out the forms, signed them, and faxed them from the Giant Eagle, where I worked. Mr. Dean gave me a selection of colors for my father's metal casket, so I chose my favorite blue shade.

On Thursday, December 28, a coworker told me that the *Canton Repository* news article report had made the national news. It seemed hard to believe, so I checked my cell phone. When I typed my name on Google News, I saw a photo of myself and the *Repository* article. I was amazed, partly because my mother often said things like I would never amount to anything when I grew up.

On January 1, 2019, my oldest daughter, Ashley, turned 26. Since Ashley and Sarah lived with their mother, I informed them about my father. Since they never knew my father, they expressed only mild interest in my dad.

I posted on Facebook that I was only about one hundred and eighty-six hours away from meeting my father. I was excited, although I had mixed emotions about not going to Dallas, Texas, to be near my father after the cemetery exhumed him. I wanted to be at the gravesite when they exhumed my dad because I had waited all my life to be with him.

A close friend helped me realize that I would not have much time with my dad after the cemetery exhumed him. I also realized that the trip would be expensive. My funeral director told me that the airport would not allow me to be near my father when the airport staff loaded his coffin onto the plane. Since my father would be transferred from his unmarked grave to the airport the same day, I understood that I would not have much time with him.

Later that day, I decided to start a Go Fund Me account to raise money to help with my expenses. I thought that people around the country would see the request. Unfortunately, I could only raise $95.00 over the next several weeks. It was discouraging when I saw that someone had raised over $5,000 to pay for their dog's medical expenses.

The next day I emailed Channel 5 News in Cleveland, Ohio. I wrote about my father and asked them if they would be interested in writing about my father and reporting on his return and burial.

On January 2, Brian Albrecht from the *Cleveland Plain Dealer* contacted me. He told me that the *Plain Dealer* had just printed his article about my dad and me. He included the only photo I had of my mother and father. I quickly went out to Giant Eagle to buy several copies of the newspaper.

On January 3, my bank gave me a bank check to pay my funeral director in Grand Prairie, Texas. He had told me that the cemetery owner would refuse to exhume my father unless he had the money by the following Monday. I hurried and mailed my payment by priority mail at the main post office in town with my father's burial set here. It upset me that the cemetery owner was so strict about getting the money. I also completed the details about my father's obituary in the *Canton Repository*.

That afternoon I received an email from Rob Powers from Channel 5 News. He told me that they were interested in telling my story. He said he was going to check with his management as to how to cover it. I was happy that the news station was interested in my account.

The following day was busy and exciting. In the morning, my funeral director at the Rossi Funeral Home emailed me and told me that he would put my father's casket into the hearse early on January 10. Then I could meet him at my church at 10:30 am with my pallbearers. We would take my father's casket into the sanctuary, and the calling hour would then be from 11 am to noon.

I received an email from the North Texas Patriot Guard Riders with a mission log. They explained how they would escort my father's casket from the funeral home in Grand Prairie, Texas, to the Dallas Fort Worth International Cemetery. Besides their organization, the local police would also supply an escort. I felt like they were treating my dad like he was someone famous.

When I went to work, a friend and coworker asked me for a copy of the two newspapers that carried the story about my dad and me. I had them with me, so I handed them to her. She said she wanted to give them to her father. Then she asked me to autograph the newspapers. I acted like I thought she was joking. Then she handed me a pen, so I signed my name in the two newspapers. I knew this feeling would not last forever, but it was nice to feel important or like a celebrity for a while. I never dreamed anyone would ask me for my autograph.

Later in the day, I emailed Rob Powers with details about my father's arrival and burial. In the evening, Rob replied that he received the final go-ahead for the story. He told me that he would interview me at my home the following Monday evening, which was the day before my father arrived in Cleveland.

I was glad that I had several days off so that I could prepare for my interview. Rob wrote that right after he got off from reporting the news at 6:30 pm Monday, he would drive from Cleveland to my home to interview me. I was very excited.

On January 5, I sent an email to the NBC News Studio in Dallas, Texas. I shared my story and informed them that American Airlines flight 2480 would fly my father's casket home on January 8, 2019. I explained that I thought they might want to report on the event.

On January 7, I went to Rittman, Ohio, to visit my mother's grave in the afternoon. I wanted to tell her that my dad was coming home.

Then, just after 6:30 pm, Rob Powers texted me that he was leaving the studios of Channel 5 News in Cleveland. I got dressed up as I did for my first photoshoot with the *Canton Repository* in December. Rob and his camera operator parked on the street near my home and walked to my front porch.

We began to get ready for my interview. This interview was different because the camera operator had other lights and moved some furnishings to get the proper lighting. I sat at my desk by my computer in my living room, and Mr. Powers sat a few feet in front of me. I was amazed that a famous news anchor from Cleveland would come to my home, because I did not live in the best part of town. The whole meeting lasted about an hour. Mr. Powers told me he would try to have a news chopper flying near the Cleveland Hopkins International Airport the following evening when my father's plane landed the next evening.

The big day

On Tuesday, January 8 2019, my youngest daughter Sarah turned seventeen. I knew that this was the day that I would finally meet my father after 65 years. In the morning, Mr. Dean emailed me to tell me that my father's body had been recovered and transported to his metal coffin. Then he sent me color photos of the entire event. On my computer that day, I saw my father's body for the first time since 1954. I could only see the body bag, but just knowing my dad was actually inside made me happy.

From the photos, I could not see a concrete liner, just dirt. There was a large concrete slab over the grave with the name BEACH written on it. The cemetery staff used a backhoe to lift my father out onto the ground. I was surprised to see that the body bag looked relatively intact after two decades.

A female medical examiner from Dallas, Texas, opened the body bag to confirm my father. Fortunately, they did not take a photo of how my dad looked. I realized that I made the right decision by not being there that morning. I decided it was best to remember my dad from the old photo rather than what he looked like after being buried for twenty years.

I had asked Mr. Dean earlier if I could have the body tag placed on my father. Unfortunately, when the medical examiner opened the body bag and looked at the label, it had turned into dust. My funeral director sent me a photo of the tag. When I saw the picture, it reminded me of a scene from a movie about the Mummy. In the film, when archeologists opened a tomb of a mummy, the body turned into dust. Only small pieces of the body tag remained.

Next, I received a phone call from the press secretary to Senator Sherrod Brown. She told me that soon the Sergeant at Arms at the U.S. Capitol Building would bring them the American flag that was flown over the Capitol to honor my father. I experienced various emotions this day.

I emailed Mr. Sereno from the *Canton Repository* to give him details about my father's funeral. The Ohio Patriot Guard Riders had arranged to meet me later that evening when I arrived. They said they would be there to honor my father.

Mr. Dean, from the funeral home in Grand Prairie, Texas, emailed me in the afternoon. He told me that at 2:56 pm, American Airlines Flight 2480 took off from Dallas Fort Worth International Airport with my father's coffin. I was glad and impressed that Mr. Dean could exhume my father and return him in just one day.

I got ready to go to the Rossi funeral home around 5:30 pm to meet my good friends Gary and Beth. The Patriot Guard Riders were there to escort us to Cleveland Hopkins International Airport. Since my interview with Rob Powers the night before, the weather conditions in Cleveland had changed. By the time I arrived at the funeral home, the rain had started up north.

I went with Gary and Beth behind the funeral hearse. The Patriot Guard Riders escorted all of us on our trip to the airport. Because of the weather conditions and cold, nobody was able to ride motorcycles. The further north we drove, the more it rained, and a weather alert was issued for Cleveland by the national weather service. Channel 5 had to ground their news chopper because of lightning. A funeral staff member told me that the airport staff said they had to delay the arrival time until 7 pm. I was disappointed because if my dad's plane had come on time, we could have returned home during daylight.

I watched the rain coming down as we drove to the airport, and I was happy that I would soon be meeting my dad. I was also frustrated that I seemed to meet so many obstacles in reuniting with my father. Even on the day I met my father, the weather was cold and rainy. A lightning storm appeared, and I wondered if my dad's plane would arrive safely.

The Patriot Guard Riders escorted us into the freight

area of the Cleveland Hopkins International Airport. I asked about being able to go to a part of the terminal to see the plane land. I learned that because it was dark, that would not be possible. After we parked, we went inside the freight office. The Patriot Guard Riders formed an honor guard line with the American Flag. I was happy to see a cameraman from Channel 5 News there.

To my left, I saw the area where they would first bring my father's casket. The office we were inside had a steel screen surrounding it that rose to the ceiling. Finally, I saw airport workers carrying my father's casket into the office area. His coffin was inside a wooden box covered by white cardboard, with an American Flag covering the top part. I had to wait a few minutes before they would bring my father's coffin to where I was.

For the first time in 64 years, I was near my father. I could not see him, but I knew that his body was only a few feet away. After waiting so long, I wanted to tear open the security door, like the "Hulk," and rush over to where my dad was. I knew it would look bad if the news station reported that security arrested me for violating security rules, so I controlled myself.

When the workers brought my father's casket into the loading dock where we were, it filled me with different emotions ranging from grief to happiness and peace. I was finally standing beside my dad. On the side of the cardboard box were the words, "HANDLE WITH EXTREME CARE." On top of the casket was an

American Flag. The Patriot Guard Riders had lined up along one side of the coffin and saluted my dad.

The funeral home staff loaded my father inside a funeral hearse, and I sat in the passenger seat. The Patriot Guard Riders went ahead of us in their cars and trucks to supply an escort home from Cleveland, Ohio, to Canton, Ohio.

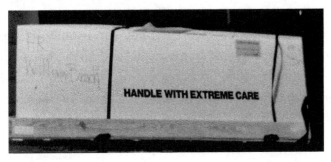

By the time we arrived back at the Rossi Funeral Home in Canton, the rain had stopped. As the hearse backed into a garage, the Patriot Guard Riders lined up along both sides. They held several American flags on both sides of the hearse.

The funeral staff placed my father's casket on a moveable cart once inside the funeral home. Then they removed the cardboard surrounding the coffin. I was amazed that an American flag was quickly placed over the casket as they removed the cardboard. They did it so fast that I could not see the casket because the flag covered both sides.

Then the funeral director told me that I could spend a few minutes with my dad before moving him inside. I looked at over a dozen veterans who were there honoring my dad, and I froze. I was afraid to show emotion or to cry because I was a man. When I grew up, men were not supposed to show emotions like crying.

I finally decided not to care what anyone thought. I touched the top of my dad's casket, and I felt a sense of peace and wholeness. I had told reporters a couple of times that a part of your heart is lost when you lose someone you love. However, you can usually fill the void with memories. In my case, I had no memories of my father because I was too young. Now that I could finally touch my father's casket, I felt like my heart was whole again.

Visiting

On January 9, 2019, I went to the Rossi Funeral Home. They had placed my father in a viewing room. I spent the afternoon with my father until the house was about to close. The room was well lit, and as I touched his casket, I knew I should be happy that we were finally together. I saw the giant American flag folded over the casket, covering it. However, I felt both happiness and sadness, knowing that I would have to say goodbye to my dad the very next day. I laid my chest on top of the casket some of the time as it was the best I could do as far as a hug.

After standing beside my father for a while, I saw Angela nearby, who was a mortician. I asked her if I could use the kneeling pew that stood close. She smiled at me and brought it over to me. I then asked her to take a picture of me kneeling beside my father's casket. Spending time alone with my father, I talked to God, and I told him that it did not seem fair. I had waited for over sixty years to meet my dad, and in less than forty-eight hours, I would have to let him go again.

A friend had told me that I had the right to open the casket to see my father. However, I knew from speaking to my funeral director in Texas that the coffin should stay sealed. The funeral director who exhumed my father told me that my father's body was more than just bones, so the casket had to be closed. I also realized that it was better to remember my dad from the one photo I had with him smiling.

The time came for the funeral home to close, so I reluctantly had to say goodbye to my father. Then I left to pick up Sarah from her mother's house to spend my court-appointed time with her. We went to the Nazarene church, which was only a couple of blocks from the funeral home where they had kept my father. After the church service was over, I took Sarah back to her mother's as I had done for the past decade. Then I returned to the home that I was renting. It was just before nine o'clock by then. Even after a decade, I still felt sad when I returned to my empty home without my youngest daughter.

However, that night I also knew that I would have to say goodbye to my father in a few hours. Unlike parting from Sarah, when I said goodbye to my dad the next day I knew I would never see his casket or touch it again. I opened my car door, and as I started to climb out, my left hand grasped the top of the door.

At that moment, I was overwhelmed by a deep sense of grief, and I remembered the song "I Can Only

Imagine" by Bart Millard. The year before, I watched the movie about Bart Millard's life several times. I thought our childhoods were similar, except in my case, it was my father who ran away and my mother who never encouraged me.

I hurried into my living room and turned my computer on. I knew it was late, but I decided to ask my pastor to play the song "I Can Only Imagine" the next day at my dad's funeral. I sent the email to my pastor. Then I decided to write down what I wanted to say at my dad's funeral service. I knew that if I got in front of people at church without a script, I would get emotional and start crying. I tried to write down some words, but I felt so much sorrow that I could not think clearly. I decided to go upstairs to take a shower. After I turned the bath shower on, the warm water poured over me, and I started to cry.

Theologians call prayer talking to God, but that night I cried out to God. I told the Lord that I just could not think of the words to say the next day. My tears mixed with the water flowing over me. I said, "Lord, I need your Holy Spirit to help me write what I want to say tomorrow. I just cannot do this on my own." After less than 48 hours of meeting my dad, I told God that I had to let him go forever. After waiting so long to be with my dad, in less than 48 hours, I would lose him again. It just felt so unfair, but there was nothing I could do.

After a few minutes, I experienced the reality of Matthew 5:4. The Bible verse says, "Blessed are those that mourn, for they shall be comforted." I got ready for bed and then went downstairs to my computer. I began to type out my eulogy for my dad. It was over six hundred words. At 11:59 pm, I posted a message on Facebook that I had finally finished my father's eulogy. Then I went to bed to get ready for the funeral just twelve hours later.

Funeral

On Thursday, I awoke early to get dressed and got ready to go to a local IHOP restaurant. I put on the only dress pants and jacket I owned. As I went outside to get into my car, I saw that it had snowed overnight. I said to myself, "You've got to be kidding me." I was frustrated because there was heavy rain and lightning when I met my dad, and now it was snowing. It seemed like obstacles to being with my dad would never stop.

I met my best friend from church, Gary, and we had breakfast together. Since my daughters were not going to be with me, it was nice to have Gary share breakfast with me. We had been friends for twenty years, and he supported me over the years after my divorce.

After breakfast, we left and went to the Church of the Nazarene in Canton. There we met my other friends who were going to be pallbearers. Then the staff of the Rossi Funeral Home came with my father's casket. One of the funeral directors and the young mortician, Angela, brought my father's coffin into the church's main entrance. Several Patriot Guard Riders lined up on both sides inside. Each of them had a large American flag beside them to honor my father. Snow covered the trees and houses outside and the roads.

I walked beside my father as they took him into the church sanctuary. After my dad's casket was in the front of the church, members of the Patriot Guard Riders lined up in front of him and saluted him. The American flag they had covered the casket with the night before was there, so I could not see the actual coffin.

We then waited around for the guests to arrive. I was disappointed that my daughters could not be with me, and I was surprised to see my ex-wife and her sister and mother come to pay their respects. I had a long table placed in the sanctuary, where I displayed my parents' photos and my father's certificates. Several of my friends from work came, and I was glad to see them.

Noon came, and everyone took their seats inside the sanctuary. I sat to the left of my father in a pew near the front. Pastor Dan Hanson invited me to come up onto the stage to present my father's eulogy.

The attendance in the usual church services numbered several hundred. I stood behind the podium and looked out into the sanctuary. I was disappointed that most of the seats were empty. With all the press coverage the past couple of months, I thought many people would come to honor my father's service to our country. I was grateful for my friends who came from work, however.

I placed my written eulogy on the podium and looked at the audience. The terrible pain that gripped me the night before was gone. I then began to read my father's eulogy out loud.

> *Today is the last day to be near my father.*
> *Tuesday was the end of a nine-year journey,*
> *or quest, to find my father, who disappeared*
> *sixty-four years ago. Now, so quickly, I must*
> *let him go away again. Then the National*
> *Cemetery will bury my father with full*
> *military honors he did not receive when he*
> *passed away from cancer on August 6, 1999.*
> *I treasure the time we had together these three*
> *days, and I know I can visit my dad. I will*
> *know where he is, but to be honest, it hurts so*
> *many words cannot describe.*

This day would not have happened without the help of Senator Sherrod Brown. He cared enough about my father to help me find my father's military records and assist with my father's remains being brought home to me.

I have often been asked why I have done this for a father who was not there for me. One reason is that I knew from the only photo I had of us that my dad loved me and was happy for me. A second reason is that he never knew it. Still, he prepared me for the time ten years ago, when my wife divorced me. Knowing what happens to a child without a father, I refused to give up on my two precious daughters.

The third and most important is that on March 6, 1972, a girl helped me walk down the aisle to the front of a church. I was too shy to go on my own, and there I asked the Lord into my heart. That night I experienced love and peace that words cannot describe. God became a father to me then. He helped me to be able to forgive both of my parents and to honor both with a military funeral.

You see, the Fifth Commandment of God does not have an escape clause. It does not say only honor your parents if they are loving and caring parents. I do not remember my mother ever telling me that she loved me. I just remember being hugged once in 1974 because my aunt told her she should before I left to go to the Holy Land.

Because of how the city of Dallas treated my father after his death, I made it my goal to have him buried in our National Cemetery. It took eight years and many setbacks, but today I honor my dad for the hero he is.

I see five qualities that made our country great starting to fade away, like the morning dew on the grass. They are honor, respect, compassion, unconditional love, and forgiveness. If we lose these qualities, we will cease to be the greatest country on earth.

Someday. I want the world to know my father's story because I believe it will encourage people to never give up on their prayers or dreams. If they keep thinking and hoping and trying, then one day, like myself, they will wake up, and what they longed for so long will become a reality.

I love my dad more than words can express, and I will cry a lot today, but this is not the end of the story but the beginning of a new one for me. My best friend, who has treated me like a brother, suggested that I write a book about my father's story. I will try because I have learned that your dreams can become a reality if you keep trying.

I stand alone today, with no other family but my father. To those of you who are here

today and honor my father for his service and
sacrifice to our great country, I call you my
family. It is an honor to have you here today.
Thank you.

I then walked back to my seat, and Pastor Hanson came and spoke to all of us. His message was not long because we were on a set schedule. Before 12:30 pm, my father's coffin was taken from the church sanctuary and placed inside the hearse. When we started to leave the service, the song "I Can Only Imagine" started to play.

I sat in the passenger seat, and Angela, the mortician, was then my driver. The city had cleared the main roads of snow, but light snow still was falling. At 12:30 pm, the Patriot Guard Riders started down Cleveland Avenue and down through the town. My dreams of citizens lining the streets paying their respects, as I had seen on YouTube, never happened, but I had my dad, and it was okay.

The National Cemetery

As we started driving, I told Angela that I was thinking about writing a book. She said that she was also thinking about writing a book. We went down through Canton city and entered the interstate on our way to Western Reserve National Cemetery. Part of our trip took us through several small towns. In a small village called Orville, we had to wait a few minutes as a train passed. I thought to myself that even today, I still had to face obstacles.

I felt sad because I would soon have to let my father go, and I would never see him again, but as we drove, I found that talking to Angela helped ease my burdens. Angela turned onto the road leading to the cemetery; I felt like all the world's cares were lifted. Seconds before we were to park, I looked to my right. I saw a cameraman standing in the grass, taking photos. I looked over at him and flashed a big smile at him. My action so surprised Angela that she laughed out loud.

We then parked by the visitor's building. Then a member of the cemetery staff came out to greet us. As I started to get out of the hearse, the reality of the day hit me again like the crisp cold air. Then Amber Moore came over to me and introduced herself. I was glad to finally meet the person who had helped make this day a reality. She told me that Senator Sherrod Brown would have the American flag flown over our nation's Capital delivered to me.

We got into our vehicles and drove down to the open pavilion for the service. Once everyone was ready, the funeral staff removed my father's casket from the hearse. They placed his coffin onto a special movable cart with wheels. Several of my friends and I looked like pallbearers, but we did not lift the casket. After entering the pavilion, we placed my father's coffin against the wall in the back of the pavilion. Six Patriot Guard Riders lined up on the left side, each holding an American flag.

I sat down on the front row of chairs with my friends Gary and Beth. Several reporters lined up along both sides of the building. Light snow was falling, and the cold wind blew throughout because the sides were open. I regretted not wearing a head covering. Several feet in front of me was my father. I tried to hold in my emotions with the press around, even though I felt sorrow because I would soon never see my dad again. While I could not see him, knowing my father was inside the casket made me feel whole inside.

A member of the armed forces stood in front of

me when it was time for the service to start. He had white gloves with a black coat and earmuffs, and he read a brief statement and then stood to the left of my father. A soldier then stood at each end of my father's casket, and they began to lift the American flag from the coffin. They carefully folded the flag according to military tradition. For the first time, I could see the entire casket. It was a bright blue with gold carvings around the sides.

The two soldiers finished folding the American flag into a triangular shape. Then one soldier came over and stood in front of me, and he knelt in front of me. He looked me in the eye and thanked me for my father's service to our country. Then he handed the American flag to me. I saw the press to my left, and I tried to hold my emotions in check, but tears did fill my eyes.

Pastor Dan Hanson came up front and stood in front of my dad's casket. After he gave his message, seven honor guard members took up their rifles just outside the pavilion. They fired off seven shots three times into the air. Then a soldier took out his trumpet from its case, and he played taps. Snowflakes fell from the sky all around us.

A member of the cemetery staff said that it was time to leave so that workers could bury my father. People started to go, but instead, I walked up to my father's casket. I clutched the American flag in my left hand and touched the coffin's top with my right hand. I knew almost everyone was gone, but I did not want to leave. I had tried so hard to be with my dad, and now I had to say goodbye forever.

At that moment, I felt a deep sense of grief. I tried to lay my chest on top of the casket, and I felt it move backward, which startled me. I knew the press was still to my left, so I put my right hand over my face, and I cried. At that very moment, a photographer from the

Cleveland Plain Dealer took a close-up photo of me to make the front page the following weekend.

I finally convinced myself that I had to let go of my father, so I turned away to leave. When I left the pavilion, a member of the honor guard presented me with a small velvet bag. Inside was the 21 shell casings from the 21-gun salute for my father.

Brian Albrecht from the *Cleveland Plain Dealer* walked up to me. He used his phone to record an interview with me that he posted on YouTube.

Before we started to leave, Pastor Hanson was talking to the funeral director and me. He shared with us that during the committal service, he had sensed the presence of my father. I thought to myself that maybe my father was an angel who visited us at the service. Unfortunately, I did not feel my dad's presence.

Afterward, I got into the car with Gary and Beth since I did not have my car. I asked them to drive me to the main office of the National Cemetery. I explained that I wanted to speak to the director to ask him if he could bury my father near my mother.

I was cleared through security to enter the office and asked to speak to the director. I explained my reason for being there. As we talked, our discussion became cordial. He mentioned that he liked Senator Sherrod Brown because he was one of only two Congressmen who helped get funding for the cemetery. He said that the area they had buried my mother in was filled.

I then discovered another mystery about my parents. He explained that he could not have a burial with my parents together; they were not married. When my mother was buried there in 2006, her marital status was listed as separated. However, the death certificate for my father listed him as divorced.

As we talked, I realized that it was not that important that the cemetery bury my father beside my mother. I had been upset that I could not see the workers bury my dad. Still, the director explained that there is no room for families to view the burial because they inter the veterans so close together. After my meeting, I traveled home with my friends Gary and Beth.

I spent my evening at home alone with my cat, Thomas. I was emotionally exhausted. I was glad that I finally gave my dad the military burial he deserved. I knew where he was, yet I still was sad because I had so little time with him.

Since I was off work for two more days, I decided to visit my father's grave the next day.

A private moment

Friday morning, I got dressed and drove back to Western Reserve National Cemetery. The snow had stopped, and the roads were clear. I parked near the visitor information center. I wanted to give them the wording for my dad's headstone, but the office was closed. The air outside was cold, but it was sunny, so I decided to find my father's grave.

The day before, people and reporters were there, but today it seemed that I was the only one around. I drove to section 10, where a map said the cemetery staff had buried my dad. They had buried my father in a new section of the cemetery. When I left my car, I could see the ground was muddy and covered with a light dusting of snow. I reached the burial site of my dad.

There was a small metal stake in the ground where they would put his headstone. It held a form that listed my father's name. I placed an American flag on the right side of my father's grave. I took a photo and posted it on Facebook. I wrote that at least this time, nobody would see me cry.

After spending some time visiting my dad and mother, I drove back home. Now that I saw where they had buried my dad, I felt at peace.

That evening when I was home, I received a text from Rob Powers from Channel 5 News. He informed me that his interview with me would air on the news at 11 pm. I was excited, so I mentioned it to my friends on Facebook and my daughters, Ashley and Sarah.

I watched the news that evening with much anticipation. During the nightly news that night on

Channel 5, they aired my interview with Rob Powers. The video was just under four minutes long. I was glad to see video clips of my time with my dad at the national cemetery. For the first time, I got to see Senator Sherrod Brown talk about my father and his funeral. I got emotional watching the video of my last moments with my father.

The next day, on January 12, I went back to work. It was less than forty-eight hours after my father's funeral. My friends at work were kind to me, which made it easier to work. I told my co-workers and customers that the *Canton Repository* and the *Cleveland Plain Dealer* would be printing articles about my dad and me the next day. I experienced various emotions at work. I still missed being with my father, but I enjoyed telling customers about my dad and my story.

After work that day, I went to a nearby Michael's craft store and bought a display case. When I got home, I put my dad's burial American flag inside the case, and I took a photo of it, which I posted on Facebook to share with my friends. I went to bed excited about what the newspapers would print about my dad and me the next day.

Sunday morning, when I went to work, I went to the newspaper stand. I was excited to see a photo and story about me on two local newspapers' front pages. I quickly bought several copies of both newspapers. I was a cashier that day, and I surprised customers when I told them I was in the newspapers. I was busy that day telling customers my story about my father and me. Several customers and friends called me a celebrity.

After work, I went to another grocery store in town to try and buy extra copies of the *Cleveland Plain Dealer*. I found a couple of issues and went to a cashier to buy them. It was then that I experienced what it must feel like to be famous. When the young cashier greeted me, she asked me how I was doing. I said that I was doing great since my photo was on the front page of the newspaper. She looked at me like I was joking. Then she looked down at the newspaper and then at me, and she looked amazed. She quickly showed the newspaper to two co-workers. The look on their faces made me feel like a celebrity.

I went back home after work very happy. I realized that fame can be fleeting and that soon the news coverage would go away. However, I enjoyed the feeling of being someone important. I suppose it was because my mother told me many times that I would never amount to much. Even after a half-century, I still had days when I felt like a failure or a nobody.

In the news

I went to work on Sunday, January 13, looking forward to reading the newspaper articles about my dad and me. I was excited and happy to see my picture on the front page of both the *Cleveland Plain Dealer* and the *Canton Repository*. Several friends and customers called me a celebrity. Being a cashier, I was able to share my story about my father throughout the day.

In the evening, when I got home, I discovered that Shane Hoover from the *Canton Repository* had shared his report with the Associated Press. I was amazed to see online that his article about me had gone viral. When I looked on Google on my computer, I noticed that newspapers around the country had carried my story. I never dreamed that people around the country would read my story. I saw that newspapers from Texas to California had reported the news about my dad and me.

That evening, I received an email from Karen, the

NBC news studio's assignment editor in Dallas, Texas. She told me that she would create a news story about my father and his funeral and asked me to send them pictures and videos of my father's funeral. Karen also informed me that she would share my father's story across all of the NBC Universal platforms, including Telemundo and Paramount pictures.

I was very excited and replied that I would try to send her photos and a short video of my father's funeral. I also emailed her a copy of the only picture I had of my parents together. I was thrilled that my story would reach so many people. I also found out that my news story made the front cover of the Military Times magazine. I was glad that servicemembers around the world could read about my father.

On Monday, January 14, I went to work and shared my story with customers when I had a chance. When I got back home, I checked my emails on my computer. Rob Powers emailed me and said he tried to email me the story he made about my dad and me. Unfortunately, the video was too large to email. He posted it on his station's website to share the video with my friends on Facebook and my daughters.

In the evening, when I was home, I typed my name and the words "world news" on Google. I was amazed to find a list of newspapers around the country that carried the story by Shane Hoover of the *Canton Repository*. I was glad that thousands of people around the country read that story about my father and me. I hoped that my account would move some of the readers to honor and respect their parents.

When I got home from work on Friday, I found an interesting letter from an attorney in Cleveland, Ohio. He told me he had recently read the *Cleveland Plain Dealer* article about my quest to find my father in his letter.

He said that my story touched him, and he contributed to Saint Joseph's Sisters in Cleveland, Ohio. He also informed me that he asked the nuns to include my parents and me in their daily prayers. I went out to a local discount store and bought a picture frame for a dollar to protect the letter because it was special.

On Saturday, a member of the NBC staff from Dallas, Texas, emailed me. She informed me she had created a news story about my dad and me and shared it with all the NBC Universal companies. Unfortunately, I never found the news story they made about me.

The third week of January came, and all the news coverage was gone. I knew this time would come, but I found myself missing telling my story to reporters. A decade of struggle to locate my dad and be with him again was now over.

Radio interview

A friend at work mentioned contacting Suzie Thomas from a local radio station in Canton. She told me that Suzie interviewed local people. On January 23, I emailed her at 95.9 The Light FM. I shared my story with her and asked if she would be interested in it. The following day Suzie replied and said she would like to interview me at her news studio.

Because of my work schedule at Giant Eagle, the earliest day Suzie Thomas could interview me was January 28. We agreed on my coming to her news station at 3 pm that day. I was excited that I had another chance to share my story and be inside a radio station. I was not worried about what to say because I had become used to being interviewed.

On Monday, January 28, I drove to the 95.9 The Light FM news station in North Canton, Ohio. A blanket of snow covered the ground, but the streets were clear. I walked into the radio station and told the receptionist that I was there to be interviewed by Suzie Thomas.

Suzie came out of her news studio to greet me. I went and sat down in her studio and waited for her to introduce me. I had never been to a radio station before, so it was an exciting experience for me. Suzie told me that she was good friends with Joe Palmisano, who did my first interview.

My interview lasted for around a half-hour, and I was relaxed and enjoyed talking. I was able to share my belief in the importance of Ephesians 6:2-3. I explained that we should honor our parents even if they had faults and that God said it would go well for us when we do. I also shared my belief that it was my mother who left and not my father.

I told Suzie that I made a discovery when I looked closely at my dad's work history. I learned that he worked in Dayton, Ohio, until I was around seven years old. I also shared that I remembered that my mother told me something that made sense when I was young. My mother said she would leave me at her parents' home when working before I started school. When I was young, I lived in a couple of different small towns about two hundred miles from where I was born in Dayton, Ohio.

I told Suzie that I believed that my mother might have kidnapped me from my father in 1954. That would explain why my mother and her family never said anything about my dad. I wondered if the reason my dad had worked over eighty jobs in sixteen states was that he was looking for me. When my interview was over, Suzie told me when she would broadcast it on the radio station.

I started to leave the studio when a young man and his family came through the entrance. He dropped off a package for Suzie Thomas, and then he went home. Suzie turned to me and asked me if I recognized him. I told her I did not. Suzie told me that he was the owner of a Christian book publishing company in southern Ohio.

I said goodbye to Suzie and started to walk to my car. Then I realized that I had not asked to have my picture taken with Suzie, so I went back into the lobby. The receptionist took a photo of Suzie and me by their station's logo. I thanked them, and then I went to work to tell my co-workers about my interview.

Now I began to adjust to the reality that my time in the spotlight had ended. I also had to get used to a life without struggle. For the past decade, I had devoted my free time to either caring for my youngest daughter, Sarah or trying to find and honor my father.

On the first day of February, I learned that Channel 5 News in Cleveland, Ohio, posted their interview on their website. I liked the title for their news story because it felt like a battle or struggle to bring my father's remains home.

On February 7, Suzie Thomas aired her two-part interview with me on 95.9 The Light FM. I let my friends and daughters know about it ahead of time. I realized that my time in the spotlight was coming to an end. For the past couple of months, I had friends and customers at work refer to me as a celebrity. I knew, though, that my story would eventually become old news, like many other news stories.

On Wednesday, March 6, I received a package in the mail. It was a special Plaque from the Patriot Guard Riders. They said that my dad was a true American hero, making me happy and proud of my father.

Moving forward

Now that I had been reunited with my father, I thought about my future. I remembered what the Apostle Paul had written about honoring our parents. He had said that things would go well with me and that I would live long. The following eight months would show me that the Apostle Paul was right.

With my daughters growing up and my father resting in peace, I decided to pursue another goal. Looking back on my life, I realized I always had a purpose or quest to seek. Now I decided to try and buy my first home, to have something tangible to leave my daughters. When my mother passed away, the only keepsake I had was a fiddle that her father had passed down to her. I learned from an old photo that my grandfather had been part of a country band and played the fiddle when my mother was a child.

For the next six months, I searched on my computer for a home that I could afford. It had taken me almost a decade to get my credit score high enough and my debt-to-income low enough to have a real chance of buying a home.

On May 23, I met with a bank loan officer in the store where I worked. He told me that I was pre-approved for a home loan. I was very excited because it meant that I could finally get serious about looking for my new home. It had taken me a decade to reach this moment. Now that I knew that I could get a home loan, I searched online for a home to buy with renewed hope.

For the next two months, I searched for homes online in the evenings after work and on my days off. I soon realized that a house that looked nice online could be quite different in person.

In the last week of July, I found what I thought was my dream home. I had a real estate agent give me a home tour, so I decided to buy it, so I offered. The following day the owner made a counteroffer which I accepted. I was excited because I believed that God had finally answered my prayers of owning my own home.

Before the sale could be completed, a home inspection was required. I had a friend, Craig, who had his own construction company. Craig and his wife, Andrea, met me at my future home. After Craig inspected the house thoroughly, he found several significant problems, like water inside the fuse box. Unfortunately, the owner refused to fix the issues or lower the price, so I decided not to buy the home.

I was discouraged, but I just started back searching again. My friend Andrea suggested a real estate agent she knew. I told my new agent what type of home I liked and quickly found some homes to look at.

I found several lovely homes, but my agent wanted me to find a home in a better location. While I searched for my new home, a loan company approved my home loan. I would still have to put a down payment. Fortunately, I qualified for help from the state of Ohio.

On Saturday, August 24, I toured a home after I got off work with my agent. After looking through the house, I told my agent that I wanted to buy the home. It had a finished basement, which I found hard to find. It was also in a safe neighborhood and near Meyer's Lake.

For most of my life, I had lived in an apartment or home that was not in a safe area. Just a couple years earlier, I rented a house on the outskirts of the city. One evening a young man was shot dead by two teenagers outside his home, which was only two doors down from me. I remembered that the Bible said life would go well if you honored your parents. Life since I gave my dad the burial he deserved seemed to be going quite well.

By the end of the month, I had signed the papers needed to buy my new home. I was surprised by how many documents were required to buy a home. This time I believed I would become a homeowner.

During the first week of September, the necessary inspections were completed. The loan company notified me that my home loan was approved and that the closing date was October 1. I was kept busy working and cleaning up the home I was renting.

On Monday, September 23, I went to meet with my agent and loan officer. I happily signed the many documents that were required. Then I officially became a new homeowner. I went to work to show my friends to share the good news.

Now that I had the keys to my new house, I started to move my belongings. On the evening of September 25, I lived out a scene from the TV *Cops* series. I had finished packing my car full of boxes and decided to cook some spaghetti for supper.

I had just sat down in my living room when I heard a knock on my front door. Since it was late, I did not open the door.

Then I heard a second knock, but nobody had said anything.

Since a neighbor, just a couple doors away, had been killed answering a knock on his door at night, I did not open my door. Then I heard a tap on my front porch window. Now I was curious, so I decided to look out the side door to my home.

When I stepped outside of my house, I saw three armed police officers staring at me. I was standing by my car, and one of the officers explained why they were there. He told me that a neighbor had called the police and reported that they thought I was moving a dead body, either inside or outside my home.

I opened my trunk and car doors and showed them

that I was not hiding a body. I told them that maybe my rolled-up sleeping bag looked like a body to a nosey neighbor. The officers were satisfied and walked away. I went back inside and had a good laugh. I wondered if I might have been shot if I had gone outside holding a spatula that I used for cooking. I was so happy to be living in my new home soon.

New home

I started to live in my new home in October. I took a couple weeks to move my belonging because I used my car instead of renting a U-Haul truck. I had no relatives except for my daughters to help me move. My friend and coworker, Brian, offered to help me with the few big pieces of furniture I had. Ironically, he had helped me a decade earlier move from my ex-wife's home into my apartment after my divorce.

For the previous four years, I had slept on a used mattress without a bed frame. A good friend from work one day told me that she had a bed frame and headboard she wanted to give me. Cheryl stopped by one day and gave them to me along with some other gifts for my home. For the first time in my life, I was a homeowner and lived in a quiet and safe place. I had a garage to park my car, a treat for me, and a large driveway.

Near the end of November, I went to the same car

dealership where I had bought my Chevy Impala. I wanted to see if I could get a new car since my credit rating was excellent. I still owed money on my old car. I was happy to learn that I qualified for leasing a new vehicle. The lease would be higher than usual because of my debt, but it was something that I could afford. For the first time in over thirty years, I now had a brand new car. It seemed that so many good things had occurred since I had shown my dad respect and honor in January.

One of the items that came with my home was an old wooden dresser left in the basement. In December, I tried to move it from the basement upstairs by myself. I thought I was being careful. I quickly discovered it was too heavy for me to move.

On December 15, after work, I felt pain in my stomach. When I went to bed, I experienced sharp pains in my stomach when I tried to lay down. I finally went to sleep after taking some aspirin.

The following Monday, I went to work because most of the pain was gone, but after standing a couple hours as a cashier, my stomach started to hurt again.

When I went on a break, my friend Sandy noticed I was hunched over. She advised me to go to an emergency room to be checked out. A manager from work drove me to a nearby emergency center. The doctor there examined me and thought my appendix was infected. He advised me to go to a hospital.

After being dropped off at a nearby hospital, I went inside the emergency room. A surgeon examined me and believed that I had a hernia. He decided to do a CT scan of my stomach. While I waited, I texted my daughters and friends on Facebook. I told them my situation and asked for prayers.

I knew I would probably need surgery, but I felt a sense of peace. I had never had a CT scan done before, and I found it "fascinating," as Mr. Spock would say. Afterward, I was taken back to my waiting room.

After a long wait, the surgeons came in and gave me the results. The chief surgeon said that my hernia was more extensive than he thought. I was also told that the scan indicated small polyps on my lungs and pancreas. My surgeon explained that my condition was severe, so he would have to do emergency surgery.

An orderly took me into a room to be prepared for my emergency surgery. Instead of feeling scared, I felt calm. My sense of humor came out when two nurses told me that I had to take my clothes off before surgery. I said to them that that was the first time a woman had asked me to drop my pants since I was married.

In a few minutes, I was wheeled into the surgery room. The room had very bright lights, and I had to look at them, being on my back. A nurse stood beside me and gave me an intravenous drip to put me to sleep. I told her I was just going to close my eyes while I waited for the surgery to start.

When I opened my eyes again, I asked the nurse when the surgery would start. I was surprised when she told me that the surgery was over. When I was in recovery, the surgeon came to see me.

My surgeon informed me that my hernia was more extensive than it appeared on the scan. He also said that my intestines had been twisted, and they had to place them back correctly. I was amazed at how they could do such delicate work.

I had to stay overnight to be watched, so I was taken to a semi-private room. I thought about my good friend, Al, that I knew from work. He was dying of cancer, and I was wondering if I also had cancer. I thought about trying to contact him, but my cell phone battery was dead. I asked a nurse if the hospital had a charging station, but they didn't.

Unfortunately, my friend Al passed away the following day.

In the afternoon, I was released to go home. My oldest daughter Ashley and her mother came to pick me up. When I started to get dressed, my nurse informed me that the staff had lost the work shirt when I arrived. I had to wear a patient gown over my pants to leave, which left part of my chest open.

When I walked into the hallway, Ashley and my ex-wife Rita commented on my clothes, so I acted like Elvis and sang a couple lines of "Burning Love." Ashley drove me home, where I had to stay for the next month.

After my first anniversary of being reunited with my father, I was able to drive. However, I had to wait a couple more weeks before working because my hernia mesh needed time to become strong enough for me to lift heavy objects.

A month after my surgery, my surgeon told me that the polyps on my pancreas and in my lungs were benign. I had been concerned, but I thought God would not let me die because I had honored my father.

Shortly after I returned to work, the Covid-19 pandemic began. I learned that I was at a higher risk because of my age. I remembered that my dad had risked his life to serve his country. I decided that this was my chance to do my part for my country by risking my life to make sure people had the groceries they needed to survive the pandemic. Throughout 2020 I continued to work and to write my life's story.

Afternote

My lifelong desire to find my father has been accomplished. However, I will still search for clues as to what happened to my half-brother and hope to someday find living relatives of my father. I also plan to write to some of the famous people I am related to, such as Prince Harry and Johnny Depp. In January of 2021, I wrote a letter to Warren Buffett. I introduced myself and my daughters to him. I told him about my father and how they were first cousins seven times removed. I included a photo of my family. The following month Mr. Buffet returned my letter. On the top portion, he wrote that it would help his reputation to be known as related to my family.

My book has reached the end, but the story of my life is not yet over. If life is like a book, then I still have new adventures awaiting me. I will have my own website to continue writing about the next chapter of my life.

I hope and pray that you will realize that you are unique and that God has a purpose for you that only you can accomplish. Our parents may not be perfect, but we need to forgive them and honor them the best possible way we can.

Never give up on your prayers or dreams. It may often take time, but you will succeed if you do not give up. There were many days in my life when things looked hopeless, and my prayers were not being answered. I held onto hope that the next day would be better. I found that certain songs would encourage me to keep going and also talking to friends.

The future awaits you, and you have the power to change your future. You cannot change your past, but you can change your future for the better. If you are interested in discovering your ancestors, you can contact me at my author website, **www.rexbeach.com**, or email **rexbeach519@gmail.com**. I love doing research and solving mysteries. Someday I hope to be able to retire and perhaps help other people learn about their ancestors.

Acknowledgements

I would like to recognize my parents, William and Helen Beach. Without them, I would not exist.

I am deeply grateful to my editor, Lin White, who is from Kent, England. Her patience and professionalism were invaluable.

As it was her divorce, my ex-wife, Rita Felty, became the catalyst for my search for my father.

U.S. Senator Sherrod Brown helped locate the evidence I needed to prove my father served in World War II. He also was instrumental in getting the State of Texas to release my father's remains from a pauper's grave.

Mr. Mark Dean of the Guerrero-Dean funeral home in Grand Prairie, Texas. His funeral service exhumed and returned my father's remains home to Ohio.

The Rossi Funeral Home in Canton, Ohio, treated my father's remains with great care and honor.

It took a decade to find and be reunited with my

father. My only relatives were my daughters then.

There were many days when my dream of meeting my father seemed hopeless because of setbacks. I was blessed to have friends at work whose encouragement and humor gave me the strength to keep trying.

I am grateful for Nancy Beddell, Sandy Abel, Steven Priest, Kim Boughman, Brian Riddell, Andrea Hill, Lisa Jenkins, Lynette Marie, Ryan Young, Bob Pflieger, Alan Riley, and Morris and Eloise DuBose.

I am very grateful to Gary and Beth Nichols, whose friendship at church helped me not give up hope after my divorce. Pastor Dan Hanson had an essential role in my father's funeral and burial.

Pam Cook and Joe Palmisano of News/Talk 1480 WHBC radio station in Canton, Ohio, gave me my first radio interview on December 08, 2018.

Dave Sereno is an editor for the *Canton Repository*. I first contacted him about my father in 2017. For almost two years, he did not lose interest in my story.

Shane Hoover of the *Canton Repository* and Brian Albrecht of the Cleveland Plain Dealer. Their news articles made my father's story known to people around the country.

Dan Deroos from Channel 19 News in Cleveland, Ohio, his on-camera interview was my first experience being interviewed inside a news station.

Rob Powers from News 5 in Cleveland, Ohio. He came to my home to do an on-camera interview the day before I met my father and recorded my reunion.

I am deeply grateful to the North Texas Patriot

Guard Riders and the Ohio Patriot Guard Riders for escorting and honoring my father's hearse and being with me during his funeral and burial.

CPSIA information can be obtained
at www.ICGtesting.com
Printed in the USA
LVHW021330151121
703325LV00005B/84